Stephanie **PARSONS**

FOREWORD BY *Kathy Collins*

First Grade

Readers

*Units of Study to Help
Children See Themselves
as Meaning Makers*

Heinemann
Portsmouth, NH

Heinemann
361 Hanover Street
Portsmouth, NH 03801–3912
www.heinemann.com

Offices and agents throughout the world

Library of Congress Cataloging-in-Publication Data
Parsons, Stephanie.
    First grade readers : units of study to help children see themselves as meaning makers / Stephanie Parsons ; foreword by Kathy Collins.
       p. cm.
    ISBN-13: 978-0-325-01728-0
    ISBN-10: 0-325-01728-X
1. Reading (Elementary).   2. Children—Books and reading.   3. First grade (Education).   I. Title.
LB1573.P28 2010
372.41'2—dc22   2010009733

Editor: Margaret LaRaia
Production editor: Sonja S. Chapman
Typesetter: House of Equations, Inc.
Cover design: Night & Day Design
Cover and chapter opening photos: Angela Jimenez
Manufacturing: Valerie Cooper

Printed in the United States of America on acid-free paper

14 13 12 11 10   RRD   1 2 3 4 5

For Huck

Contents

Foreword by Kathy Collins vii

Acknowledgments ix

Introduction 1

Chapter 1   Becoming a Community of Readers 8

Chapter 2   Making Sense of Those Little Black Marks 28

Chapter 3   Bringing Books to Life 53

Chapter 4   Reading with a Wide-Awake Mind 70

Chapter 5   Reading to Learn 93

Chapter 6   Sounding Like Readers 117

Chapter 7   Planning for Independence and Summer Reading 136

Appendix A: Student Handouts 147

Appendix B: Websites to Help Foster Reading 153

Foreword

In Japanese workplaces, new, or junior, employees (*kohei*) are usually teamed up with a senior employee (*sempai*). The *sempai* assumes the role of mentor, introducing the *kohei* to the culture of the company and helping her to fit in smoothly and seamlessly with the team. The *sempai* also acts as a confidant and supportive sounding board to the *kohei* as she shares her struggles and worries. Although they arrange formalized appointments to meet at work, many moments of *sempai/kohei* relationship building take place during after-hours karaoke sessions, usually in between Beatles' songs.

Back some years ago, as I was about to start another year as a first grade teacher at PS 321 (a school in Brooklyn, not in Japan), Stephanie Parsons was beginning her first year there, also as a first grade teacher. Our principal informally teamed up the new teachers with a more experienced teacher on staff, and I was asked to be *sempai* to Stephanie, my *kohei*.

We talked often in those early days. We visited each other's classrooms as we set them up in August. I envied Stephanie's mod Ikea bookshelves and her ability to set up a classroom in a way that made it work efficiently, yet still feel warm and pleasant. Once the school year began, we talked about our teaching and our students, sharing stories of first grade drama and trauma.

As her *sempai*, I gave Stephanie crucial information about the top secret location of the school's nonprimary color construction paper stash, I whispered advice about how to deal with the moody custodian, and I offered suggestions about how to talk with a particularly challenging parent about a particularly sensitive issue. As her *sempai*, I watched Stephanie take snippets of conversation between children and make them into teachable moments. I listened closely as she talked about her innovative teaching ideas. I envied her self-made plan book. It wasn't very long before I realized that this wasn't going to be a typical *sempai/kohei* situation. Even though I was supposed to be the mentor, I quickly knew that I would be learning quite a lot in this relationship. That's the nature of time spent with Stephanie—you learn a lot, and you laugh a lot.

With *First Grade Readers*, you have the wonderful opportunity to spend time with Stephanie, and you, too, will learn a lot and laugh a lot. As you read, let Stephanie become your reading workshop *sempai*. Let Stephanie take you (and your students) on the journey of a comprehensive, yet well-paced, year of reading workshop. Read closely as she shares brilliant ideas for creating a robust, child-friendly reading workshop characterized by high expectations and plentiful learning opportunities.

By providing a clear vision of a year of first grade reading, Stephanie makes reading workshop seem very possible to implement . . . immediately. Stephanie shares teaching ideas and specific suggestions for units of study that focus on accuracy, fluency, comprehension, genre, and independence. Throughout, she helps us reimagine possibilities for familiar units while also introducing ideas for innovative units.

Stephanie's writing, like her classroom and her teaching, is crisp, clean, and efficient, yet also warm and welcoming. The units are presented in an intuitive and focused way, making everything feel as if it's within reach, no matter if you're a brand-new teacher beginning your first year or a veteran teacher with lots of workshop teaching experience, no matter if you're a teacher in an urban school with a concrete playground or a teacher at a rural school with an unobstructed view of the horizon.

In addition to compelling units of study, Stephanie also teaches us about the culture of a healthy, vibrant reading workshop. As you read, you'll notice the language of invitation, the act of demonstration, and the power of opportunity—Stephanie's teaching is infused with words that invite young readers to imagine themselves reading the best they can and demonstrations for exactly how to do that; and words that invite students to read, think, and talk together about books with growing sophistication, and opportunities for book talks that push young readers to think, and then to outgrow their thinking.

In her role as our reading workshop *sempai* in *First Grade Readers*, Stephanie doesn't only mentor us to teach first graders how to read with power and joy; she also shows us how to teach with power and joy. Thank you, Stephanie. We need this now.

—Kathy Collins

Acknowledgments

The longer I work in this field, the more amazing, thoughtful, inspiring, and just plain nice people I meet. All of these people contribute to my thinking about teaching, whether or not they mean to, and whether or not our interests are the same. The world of reading and writing instruction is a big one, but this community feels like a family of sorts for me.

I am forever indebted and grateful to Lucy Calkins. I knew her first as a graduate student, then as a teacher growing through the support of the Teachers College Reading and Writing Project, and finally as a staff developer in that organization. In all of these roles, I learned more than I would have thought possible about teaching children to read and write well. Her encouragement and acknowledgment have been invaluable.

I have the enormous good fortune to be part of a community of thinkers, writers, teachers, and friends in this field who have been a huge influence on the way I think about children's literacy. Carl Anderson helps me work through issues and ideas in my work with great clarity. Ralph Fletcher is one of the kindest and most encouraging mentors a girl could have. Talking with him always helps me see reading and writing as something much bigger and juicier than just what we do in classrooms, which then makes my work in classrooms bigger and juicier. My conversations with Tom Newkirk have been most important to me as the mother of a young boy, and have influenced the way I think about teaching all children. Katherine Bomer approaches her work so lovingly and respectfully. When I get to spend time with her, I try to drink up as much as I can of her joyful intelligence and depth. My conversations with Randy Bomer always leave me with a sense of clarity and purpose about my work with literacy. I can't figure out how he finds the time to be so aware of what is going on in all quarters of current research and still be so creative with his own work. Isoke Nia, my first staff developer, shaped my work from the very beginning, teaching me how to trust children to know and be able to do so much more than I thought they could. She saw something in me that I didn't know was there, and I'm so grateful to her for letting me in on it. Katie Wood Ray taught me so much about the delicate act of guiding children to discover rather than imposing my teaching upon them. She was the first person to encourage me to write books like this one, and I'm eternally grateful that she did. I hope you'll see the watermark left by each of these people within the pages of this book.

I owe so many thanks to all of my colleagues at the Teachers College Reading and Writing Project. A few years ago I was sitting around talking with my friends, Amanda Hartman and Shanna Schwartz, about reading with children and that elusive quality of engagement. This conversation became an informal study group, all of us exploring ideas with children and getting together to talk about it. We kept discovering that when they had more ways to engage with a text, children engaged more deeply, and that this made children's comprehension more sophisticated. Some of what you see in this book, particularly in the unit on dramatization, "Bringing Books to Life," came directly out of this conversation. I feel so lucky to have been part of these conversations. Cory Gillette is first a friend, the best kind a person can have, and I'm thankful to her just for that. She also happens to be incredibly knowledgeable about reading. When I needed to broaden my knowledge beyond my comfort zone of primary reading, I went to Cory. Her tutorials about reading in higher grades have been not only fascinating but also so vital to my understanding of the whole spectrum of reading instruction. Even though this book is about first grade readers, it is written with a strong knowledge of where children need to go next as readers. I owe this knowledge to Cory.

I have had the pleasure to work with many gifted and inspiring teachers over the years. I could not have written this book without the challenging conversations, thoughtful suggestions, and willing implementation of the teachers I worked with this year. Seth Phillips, principal of P.S. 8 in Brooklyn, welcomed me into his school for years, giving me a special home and a warm community. Staff development can be lonely work sometimes, and a school like this is a gift. Sandy Long, Aleah Forrest, and Jessica Levy were three first grade teachers who modified their calendars in order to pilot many of the units in this book. Their talented teaching and insightful feedback were vital to my writing. Special thanks go to the first grade team at the Coman Hill Elementary School in Armonk, New York: Elizabeth Courtney, SuAnn Dorfman, Lisa Jacobsen, Maureen Lavin, Susan Liebman, Kathryn Meaney, Sue Ornstein, Kirstin Russell, Stephanie Adler, Susan Tyrrell, and Heather Nimsger, and their fabulous literacy coaches, Elana Levy and Sandy Levin, and of course their wonderful principal, Carol Fisher, who made it all possible.

Kate Montgomery has been my friend since we were teenagers. She brought me to teaching and to Teachers College. Her humor, warmth, love, and encouragement supported me through plenty of difficult times. She edited my other books and got this one started, despite a demanding (and well-deserved) promotion. Her knowledge and insight are a rarity and I'm so glad I get to be on the receiving end as often as I do. Over the years, Kate's friendship has been a true gift.

I first met Ginny Lockwood when my designated cooperating teacher was put on bed rest for her pregnancy and I found myself student teaching with a substitute who himself had barely taught. Ginny welcomed me into her classroom, and I knew in about two seconds that my misfortune had suddenly turned into a winning lottery ticket. Ginny is one of the most gifted teachers I know, and she is so giving with her knowledge and expertise. In the years since we first met, I have been reminded many times of Ginny's intelligence and generosity. Whenever I feel like I need to expand my knowledge or grow my confidence about literacy, I ask Ginny for advice. Not only will she tell me the smartest things, but she'll do it with impressive depth and breadth. I am so lucky to know her and I only hope I can give back half of what she gives me.

Aah, the illustrious and amazingly kind and humble Kathy Collins. It doesn't get any better for a first year teacher than teaching down the hall from Kathy! She knows so much about teaching reading and is willing to sit and talk through all of it with a friend. Kathy approaches her work with a healthy sense of humor and yet an uncompromising intelligence. It was such an obvious and natural choice to ask Kathy to write the foreword for this book, and I couldn't have been more honored that she accepted.

The fantastic and amazing Heinemann team is almost entirely responsible for this book. I'm pretty sure I did the easy part! Cindy Black is a hero who shouldn't be unsung. Without her this book would be three times as long and not nearly as clear and consistent. Sonja Chapman made sure all of the various pieces of this book fit together exactly as they should, in the clearest and prettiest possible way. I sincerely appreciate the hard work of Eric Chalek. He pays attention to you, dear reader, and gets the book you need into your hands. In this case, it was my book! Many thanks again to Kate Montgomery, publisher extraordinaire, for lighting the fire that made this book actually happen. My brand-new editor, Margaret LaRaia, had a tall order with this one. She stepped into this project midstream and handled the job remarkably well. Her comments and suggestions were always well timed, apt, relevant, encouraging, informative, helpful, and everything else an overwhelmed writer needs them to be. She always understood what I was trying to say and helped me say it in the best and clearest way.

I owe so much to my parents and four siblings, the very first teachers and readers I knew. Each of them reads in a different way, and through their example, I learned not just how to read but also how to have an identity as a reader. Very special thanks is reserved for Christina Kelly, who gave me the time and space I needed to get into a chair and put words onto paper. She was there to listen when I needed to talk through ideas. Her contribution to this project has been huge. Finally, thanks to my son, Huck, who has read with me every day since he was born and has even started to read *to* me.

Introduction

Recently I watched my two-year-old son read *Go, Dog, Go,* by P. D. Eastman. He stared intently at a page for a while, and then turned to stare at the next page. Sometimes he smiled, pointed to something, made a face, or said some of the words of the text. He kept himself occupied like this long enough for me to fold a whole basket of dark laundry.

It gives me great pleasure so see Huck so engaged with reading on so many levels, especially given that he's not actually decoding any of it. Engagement with reading has come so naturally to him that I sometimes wonder if formal instruction is going to compromise this. As a teacher, I see children who had previously loved to read become anxious about reading in school. Somehow school reading feels surrounded by benchmarks and levels, rather than by joy and abandon. I wish I could bottle whatever it is Huck's doing and pour it into every primary classroom I visit.

This book is the best way I know how to do just that. Experience has shown me (and research supports it) that reading achievement improves not with increased testing but with increased reading—and not just any reading, but repeated reading of relatively easy to decode, interesting, self-selected texts. These are the texts that children most want to engage with deeply, and you can show them the way.

The seven units in this book develop children's ability to decode and understand a variety of texts. The first unit, on setting up a strong community, supports the work in the remaining units—"Making Sense of Those Little Black Marks," "Bringing Books to Life," "Reading with a Wide-Awake Mind," "Reading to Learn," "Sounding Like Readers," and "Planning for Independence and Summer Reading." Each unit focuses on a different aspect of reading, all of which work together to foster complete readers. Figure I-1 is one possible calendar showing how all these units can work together.

The units in this book deal with the reading skills I most want to share with you, but they are not the only choices! I did not, for example, include a unit introducing the concept of books clubs. You may want to create such a unit of study of your own based on your needs and those of your students. If you do, I highly recommend Kathy Collins's amazing book *Reading for Real*. With tremendous clarity, Kathy will inspire you to lead your children to great places in their reading, thinking, and talking. And while I'm on the subject of Kathy Collins, her book, *Growing Readers*, is a must-have resource for any primary teacher.

In choosing which units of study to teach, we must consider balance, standards, our favorite literature, and the life of our classroom. A curriculum needs balance. Some units will be genre based (nonfiction, for example), while others will focus on a skill (perhaps fluency). We may also want to vary the

SEQUENCE AND TIMING	UNIT OF STUDY
1 (September-October)	Becoming a Community of Readers
2 (October-November)	Making Sense of Those Little Black Marks
3 (December)	Bringing Books to Life
4 (January-February)	Reading with a Wide-Awake Mind
5 (March-April)	Reading to Learn
6 (May)	Sounding Like Readers
7 (June)	Planning for Independence and Summer Reading

Figure I–1 Possible Calendar for Reading Workshop

pace, following long units with short ones and vice versa. Of course, our curriculum must also address the requirements set forth by our school, district, or state. Then, too, we should all be allowed to teach what we love, if for no other reason than to model for children how loving something makes it more fun to learn about it. Finally, the life of the classroom should be a factor in some curriculum decisions.

■ How the Units Are Set Up

Every unit of study in this book is presented in a similar way: a brief overview followed by a more detailed description of the steps in planning and teaching it. These steps are discussed below.

Setting Goals

The goals for each unit are divided into four categories: *making meaning, decoding, habits,* and *community*. These goals take into account not only children's ability to decode and comprehend but also some other beliefs about young readers, namely that our classes must be communities and our children must become independent if they are going to read for life. Deciding the goals of any given unit of study can be difficult. As teachers, we want to teach it all at the same time. It's hard to wait to teach something that we wish our kids could do now. That's why this step is so important. We *can't* teach it all at once! We have to set goals for each unit that are realistic and that build on the work of prior units so that we are able to teach it all by the end of the year.

Getting Ready to Teach

Before we begin a new unit of study, we need to prepare physically and mentally for the demands posed by the curriculum. We must identify and gather the materials we will need and think about what lessons will be best for these particular children. The next step is considering the children, reflecting on the unit that came before, looking at how we guided our students toward the goals we set there, and planning how we will continue to guide them toward the goals of the next unit. Once you have gathered materials and considered your students, you are ready to prepare demonstration materials. Look through the teaching ideas in the unit and think about which books work best as tools for practicing the skills required. Some texts can be used as they are, but others may need to be prepared in some way, by enlarging a page, covering or highlighting parts of the text, or writing sticky notes. The more of this you prepare ahead of time, the more smoothly the lessons will go.

A Note on Demonstration

Demonstrating makes all the difference. When teaching skills or strategies, we need to keep in mind that we are not modeling but demonstrating. Demonstrating is more deliberate and focused and has certain qualities that make it an effective method for teaching strategies. The important principles of a demonstration are:

● One thing is being demonstrated or highlighted. A demonstration is most clear when the skill or strategy being taught is clearly defined. If a strategy has more than a handful of steps or is too elaborate, it needs to be broken down. It can be difficult, but we must strive to name the strategy or skill being taught in every lesson. We want students to know what they are about to learn, but we also know that putting a strategy into words forces us to be clear and succinct about what that strategy actually is and how it can be done. For example, *being a good partner* cannot be clearly demonstrated. It is vague and means different things to different people on different days. The small steps that children need to take to become good partners, though, can be demonstrated. *Sitting hip-to-hip with the book between you* can be shown clearly and unambiguously in the space of a few minutes.

● The demonstration is accompanied by a verbal description. A demonstration without an accompanying description of the action is like magic. We watch the trick and are impressed and amazed but could not possibly repeat it on our own. The purpose of this accompanying description is to demystify the process of reading and writing by sharing our insiders' knowledge. Imagine the magician telling his audience, "There's a hidden compartment here and that's where I get the second coin. See?" Some people call this verbal description *thinking aloud,* a phrase that aptly implies a private viewing into the mind of the expert. We are naming and describing a process that has become second nature to us but is still a challenge for our students.

● The language is clear and consistent. While thinking aloud, we must remember to use language that children understand. Too many metaphors or digressions will cloud the process rather than make it clear. Where possible, we must use consistent language to describe the strategies we are demonstrating. If we say sometimes, "Sound it out," and sometimes, "Get your mouth ready," and sometimes, "Think about the sound that letter makes," it can be confusing. It is easier to cue children to use a strategy when we describe that strategy with a consistent phrase.

■ Teaching the Units

Each unit is divided into sections of related teaching ideas. It helps children learn the larger concepts we want to teach if we spend several days focused on each one before moving to the next one. Within each section of a study, you will find guiding questions and topics for lessons, conferences, or mid-workshop focus points. Guiding questions help frame a study by launching a conversation for the community to participate in. The questions might not have immediate answers, and many of them have a variety of possible answers.

The topics for lessons, conferences, or mid-workshop focus points are teaching ideas you will need to address in different ways depending on your class. Most units suggest more teaching points than there are days recommended. This is to give options based on the many different kinds of first grade class and to allow you the final decision in what *your* class needs most.

- If a teaching point seems right for half to three-quarters of your class, teach it as a lesson, preferably with a strong and clear demonstration.

- If just a few children need to work on a teaching point, individual conferences may be the best place to address it.

- If a teaching point seems just right for either a more novice or more advanced subset of children, teach it to them as a small-group lesson.

- If children are somewhat familiar with an idea, or it is not a tricky concept for them, you might want to introduce it simply as a reminder or a mid-workshop focus point, in which you stop the whole class during their independent reading time and remind students of a particular reading behavior.

- If nobody seems ready yet for a teaching idea, write it on a sticky note and put it into the next chapter. When you get to that chapter, reevaluate that lesson's appropriateness.

- Finally, there will be teaching ideas that just don't work for every class every year. I wrote these ideas based on many years of teaching in scores of classrooms. A year of teaching reading shouldn't look identical to every other year of teaching reading because the classes are never identical.

Reflecting and Celebrating

This is included in every unit. Sometimes as children share their work, and usually at the end of a unit, we need to encourage students to reflect on their learning. We might ask them questions orally or in writing. The major things we want to know are what students say they have learned, what they think they have done well, and perhaps what was difficult for them. This tells us whether we are getting our point across and helps us understand how the children perceive our teaching. More important, it encourages the children to find words to describe what they are learning to do as readers. When they can name their intentions, it becomes possible for them to judge for themselves whether they are successful. Their decisions are now motivated from within, not from us. This done, we are ready to celebrate! This is the reward for all our hard work.

Celebrating is not just for writing workshop, and not every celebration has to have balloons and parents and cupcakes. Most, in fact, will be simple and intimate: just the students gathering in a circle and sharing important discoveries in their reading or offering compliments to classmates. We may make a toast with a cup of juice, congratulating ourselves for the achievement and launching ourselves into the next challenge. Of course, sometimes (maybe twice during the year) we will want to pull out all the stops and invite the children's families and the school community to share in the joy and pride that comes from a job well done.

Celebrations shouldn't be skipped. Even a small celebration is important to the future of our reading communities. A celebration at the end of a unit of study is akin to graduation. We acknowledge and validate the progress we have made and name the new skills we have mastered or at least begun to master. We also prepare mentally for a new unit, unknown territory into which we can venture with the certainty that all our efforts will be rewarded with new learning. Celebrating is a way to help us be aware of our learning, and it helps children follow our lessons more fearlessly than they otherwise might.

■ Checking In

The end of each unit is a good time to check in with the goals of that unit. You will have an opportunity to decide if some of the teaching ideas need to be taught again to the whole class or reviewed with small groups or individuals.

First graders are amazing. Watching them become readers is one of the great gifts of this job. This year, with your help, they will put together the pieces of decoding, thinking, feeling, understanding, and responding to perform the feat of reading. I hope these units provide the rigorous curriculum you want and the fun you need to guide your students toward a lifelong love of reading.

■ Professional Resources

Calkins, Lucy. 2001. *The Art of Teaching Reading*. New York: Addison-Wesley Educational Publishers.

Collins, Kathy. 2008. *Reading for Real: Teach Students to Read with Power, Intention, and Joy in K–3 Classrooms*. Portland, ME: Stenhouse.

———. 2004. *Growing Readers: Units of Study in the Primary Classroom*. Portland, ME: Stenhouse.

1

Becoming a Community of Readers

I am a reader. I always have a book or two going and one or two more waiting in the wings. I read a variety of stuff—classics, mainstream best sellers, nonfiction, fiction, memoir, newspapers, blogs, literary magazines, junk. So it came as an unpleasant surprise when, after my son was born, I stopped reading. I didn't really realize it was happening. I was too caught up in this amazing new little person in my life and all of our daily miracles and discoveries.

When the fog of new motherhood started to clear, I realized I missed my reading life. I missed the connections of reading—connections to the world, certainly, but mostly connections to people. I was no longer able to participate in discussions about a new book, a story in *Harper's*, or even current events. I couldn't say, "Yes, I know what so-and-so has to say about such-and-such, and here's what I think about it. What do you think about it?" Without this dialogue, my thoughts seemed so small. And lonely.

Of course, my universe was made exponentially bigger by Huck being in it now. My maternity leave from the rest of the world had other blessings, too. One is that I have a new appreciation for the time I am able to spend reading, and for the time I am able to spend talking with others about what I'm reading. This includes reading to and with Huck, by the way! An unexpected blessing is a deeper appreciation of the power of reading to bring people together so that we can have ideas that are greater than the ones we might have had alone. If I hadn't lost this for a while, I wouldn't have known how much I depend on it. I do not think that we have to talk about every single thing we read in order to derive meaning from it, but I would go so far as to say that reading is a basic need for a community. I believe that we must invite children to become a community of readers early—before they even think of themselves as readers.

■ Overview

In my vision of a community, children:

- are willing to take risks and try new things

- want to read every day

- see their daily reading as something that benefits them (rather than as something you want from them)

- are moved by what they read

- cooperate in maintaining a productive and safe environment

- may be reading different kinds of texts on different levels from one another

- know and care about what their classmates are working on

- comment thoughtfully on one another's ideas

- value one another's efforts

The ideal conditions for a community like this to flourish are time, patience, and a willingness to give up a little control. We must also be mindful of the way we use language, phrasing our thoughts in a way that lets children know they share ownership of the community. Instead of, "I asked you to keep it quiet in here," we might say, "I thought what you said about needing a quiet classroom was so important that I'll do whatever it takes to help you get it, even if that means stopping you five times during reading workshop!" Subtle shifts like this make a big difference.

The purpose of this unit is to establish a strong classroom community, one that operates smoothly and in which children feel safe to take risks. This takes about four or five weeks. Start by creating an environment where everyone can succeed, regardless of prior experience with reading. This means letting children know there are lots of different kinds of readers and there is room for all of them in your classroom.

You will then need to spend a lot of time setting up routines—physical routines, such as getting and returning books, as well as mental habits, such as thinking about books. It's easy to write this down in the peace of my little room, much harder actually to do. Your lessons might not follow a typical structure, and you may find yourself repeating the same direction many times. With consistency and determination, it will fall into place. At the end of the unit, ask children to reflect on their progress this month, sharing what they've learned. An intimate celebration is probably in order, too, as you all will deserve some congratulations for a month of hard work!

■ Goals/Outcomes

You have big goals for this year, some of which will be achieved in particular units of study, others that will be reached by the end of the year. In order to teach the amazing and wondrous art of reading, though, you will have to lay some serious groundwork. The goals of this unit have not so much to do with reading *skills* as they have to do with building good reading *habits*. As in the rest of the units, the goals here fall into four categories.

Making Meaning

We hope children will

- share favorite books with peers
- show engagement with reading material
- say what books are mostly about

Decoding

We hope children will

- use pictures as a source of information while reading
- identify word wall words (words that have been taught separately) in their books

Reading Habits

We hope children will

- choose books thoughtfully

- handle books carefully

- get to and from the meeting area quickly and quietly

- stay productive for about fifteen to twenty minutes (by the end of the unit; this includes partner and private reading time)

- talk about their books

Community

We hope children will

- discuss books with partners

- participate in lessons and discussions

- respect the range of abilities in the class

- treat other readers' time, ideas, and space with respect

◾ Getting Ready to Teach

As summer nears its end, I find myself mentally preparing to get back to work. I look at the children's names and read last year's teachers' comments. I make a million labels and lists with their names, imagining their personalities as I type them in. I gather the books I will need to draw these children into the mysterious and wondrous world of reading. I collect what I'll need to demonstrate the behaviors and strategies I want to teach.

Gathering Materials

I usually have to reorganize my classroom library twice during the school year. The first time I set it up, before children actually come to school, should last until December with only minor modifications. I put out baskets of books organized by level and by other principles (friendship, homes, animals, nonfiction, poetry, etc.) and containing a variety of levels. I put out the levels I need according to all the assessment data I have—usually levels A to H, but often I need a few higher books for just one or two children. For the first two or three weeks of school, I may have part of my classroom library blocked off. I don't want children to be overwhelmed by the quantity of books in the classroom, and there will be plenty of time during the year to explore all of the books.

One of the supplies I ask parents for is gallon-sized resealable plastic bags. These will become children's book baggies. (You can also use magazine bins or any other container you like.) I give each student one for school and one to take home each night. By the end of the first unit, I have introduced both. In the meantime, children read each day from bins of books. I compile one bin for each table, including a variety of levels, genres, and topics. I rotate the bins every day so that children have different books to look at while I get to know them as readers. At the end of the week, I change the books for the following week. These bins help with management, also, by making it interesting for children to stay in their seats during reading. By the time they get their individual baggies, I will have taught them how to move about the room and to choose books effectively.

Considering Students

You may or may not know very much about your students before school starts. The information that may help the most in setting up your classroom concerns attitudes, tastes, and levels. This will help you fine-tune the decision of which books to put into bins at the start of the year and how to organize your library to draw students toward its many charms. If you can't get much information about students' likes and dislikes before school starts, try organizing part of the library (not the leveled part, but the part sorted by topic, theme, or genre) with the children in the first week of school. You need ways to fill time while their reading stamina is still so short, and this can help them develop a sense of ownership and shared purpose toward the library. It may seem overwhelming to allow children into the room without everything organized, but it can be so much fun to watch what happens when children think about how to label and fill baskets of books:

> "Let's have a whole basket about transportation, like trains and airplanes and stuff!"

> "OK, but what about trucks that do stuff, like fire trucks or bulldozers? Do those go in the transportation bin?"

> "We could have it be 'things that go' instead of 'transportation.'"

These negotiations never cease to amaze and entertain me. Of course I'm right there ready to mediate when necessary, but even that creates an opportunity for children to learn.

Preparing Demonstration Materials

In this unit, you demonstrate behaviors and routines more than reading strategies. This means you show children how you would like them to move around the room, get and return materials, treat books and one another, and participate in lessons and conferences. You need not prepare any special materials for this, but you will want to have your room and library set up to facilitate orderly usage and movement. I have suggested a few lessons in this unit that give children some basic print and engagement strategies so they have a way into their books as they learn the routines. For these lessons, you may want to prepare a couple of books so you can show children exactly what you hope they will do independently.

Choosing Texts to Help You Teach

When choosing books to support your work in this unit, for read-aloud, lesson demonstrations, or shared reading, look for books with a strong community message. Some suggestions follow.

- Books about the joys and pains of friendship, such as
  - *My Best Friend* by Mary Ann Rodman and E. B. Lewis
  - *The Hating Book* and *Let's be Enemies* by Charlotte Zolotow
  - *Best Friends* by Miriam Cohen
  - *Enemy Pie* by Derek Munson and Tara Calahan King

- Books about respecting and appreciating all kinds of people, such as
  - *I Love My Hair* by Natasha Anastasia Tarpley and E. B. Lewis
  - *The OK Book* and *The Peace Book* by Todd Parr
  - *Odd Velvet* by Mary Whitcomb and Tara Calahan King

- Books about school and school-related anxiety, such as
  - *The Recess Queen* by Alexis O'Neill and Laura Huliska-Beith
  - *First Grade Takes a Test* and *Will I Have a Friend* by Miriam Cohen and Ronald Himler
  - *When Will I Read?* by Miriam Cohen and Lillian Hoban
  - *Wilson Sat Alone* by Debra Hess and Diane Greenseid

Don't forget to read some books purely because they are fun or funny!

■ Teaching

We Are All Readers

Sending a letter to students and their families a couple of weeks before school starts is a time-honored ritual of August. In my letter, along with the requisite supply list, I write a note to caregivers briefly outlining my hopes and dreams for the year, inviting them to share theirs with me. I also include a note to the children telling them how lucky I feel to be their teacher and how much fun we are going to have and anything else I can think of to help ease their anxiety. I also ask them to bring their favorite book to school on the first day. If it's a book they don't own, I invite the parents to tell me so I can try to get my hands on a copy.

This book is the centerpiece of the first section of the study. It acts as a sort of security blanket on that crucial first day, and quickly becomes an icebreaker, a friend maker, and a chance for the teacher to take a breath! If you can't swing this, I highly recommend borrowing a few favorite books from the kindergarten teachers, so children enter the room already familiar with some great books. You want children's first impression of reading workshop to be, "I can hardly believe my luck! We get to read every day, and such great books with such fun friends! I bet I can get good at this!" You can introduce the rules and routines later, after children have decided reading workshop is a good thing.

Guiding Question

● *What do we need in place in order to do our best reading work?* By asking children this question, you invite them to participate in charting the course your year will take. You want them to help you create a set of principles by which the class will operate. They will probably say many of the same things you would say if you were laying out the rules for them, such as, "We need to treat one another nicely." Asking for their input is a way of putting your money where your mouth is when you tell them you'd like to create a community. You will need to attend to the language you use, rephrasing children's ideas as necessary. If they suggest reading be silent, for example, you might respond, "Well, maybe we should say that reading is pretty quiet, because a lot of us like to read with our voices."

Topics for Lessons, Conferences, or Mid-Workshop Focus Points

● *We're so lucky we get to read every day in this class. A good way to start is to share a favorite book with a new friend.* When I teach something new, I like

TIME FRAME	SECTION OF STUDY	WHAT CHILDREN DO	WHAT WE TEACH
2–3 days	We are all readers	• Begin to get to know the individuals who make up the community of readers • Begin to think of themselves and one another as readers	**Guiding question** • What do we need in place in order to do our best reading work? **Topics for lessons, conferences, or mid-workshop focus points** • We're so lucky we get to read every day in this class. A good way to start is to share a favorite book with a new friend. • A great way to share books is to talk about what it's like to read it at home. • It's good to know what makes reading go well for us.
10–15 days	Readers have routines	• Learn and practice the predictable routines of reading workshop • Get used to working in the community of readers who make up this particular class • Learn some ways to stay productive, even if they are not yet confident readers	**Topics for lessons, conferences, or mid-workshop focus points** • Readers treat their books with loving care. • Readers choose books they think they can spend some time with. • Readers move around the space quietly so as not to distract other readers. • Readers find out as much as they can about their books before they start reading. • A book's repeated pattern can make it easier to read. • Readers look at the words they're reading, even if they know them by heart (they may even point to each word with a finger). • Readers get stronger by spending time with the same books. • Sometimes it's good to read with a partner. The way to do this is to move your chair or body to be sitting next to one another. • Readers sometimes have a special place to read. • One way to stay productive during reading workshop is to reread your book, trying to make it sound nice and smooth. • One way to stay productive in reading workshop is to find a page in your book you'd like to show your partner. • If you get to a tough word in your book, see if the picture can help you. • If someone near you is distracting you, give a gentle reminder of how reading workshop goes.
2 days	Reflecting and celebrating	• Think about and celebrate how much they have grown in the first month of school	**Guiding questions** • How are we more grown up as readers now than we were on the first day of school? • What questions or compliments do you have for one another about your reading growth?

Figure 1–1 Unit at a Glance

to start by building up a lot of enthusiasm. The first day of reading workshop in your classroom leaves a strong first impression with your students of what learning to read feels like. You probably want it to feel fun, safe, and comfortable. If you asked your students to bring a favorite book to school on the first day, now is the time to pull it out and share it with a new friend. Use this time to observe how children interact with their books: Do they flip through quickly? Do they find a favorite page and pore over it? Do they read conventionally? Do they make up a story to go with the pictures? Do they share? This information helps you assign temporary partners and reading spots, if you choose to.

- *A great way to share books is to talk about what it's like to read it at home.* This idea continues to highlight the connection of reading with a place of comfort. You may ask children to talk to one another about reading at home, or you can even have them draw a time when reading feels good. The more opportunities we give children to think of themselves as readers, the more confidence they have in their own ability to learn. Children may choose a book, either from home or from your classroom library, to read. To extend the time, give students a chance to talk to a partner or friend about what reading is like at home. At the end of the workshop, partners can share about one another: "I read with Jonathan today, and he's the kind of reader who likes to stop and talk about the story while he reads."

- *It's good to know what makes reading go well for us.* As a reader, sometimes things go well for me and sometimes they don't. I like to read before going to sleep, I like to read on subways and airplanes, and I like to read on vacation. I can read with certain kinds of noise, but others make it impossible. I cannot read when I am anxious. Knowing these things about myself helps me choose when, where, and even how to read. I ask my first grade students to be reflective of their reading from the very beginning. I want to know when reading feels good for them, and also when it feels not so good. Just getting them to think about reading in this way is part of my goal. I also take note of what makes reading feel good for them so I can create conditions in the classroom that help them find that feeling. I may jot down or chart their responses, asking them on a later date how we can make our classroom as much of a good-feeling reading place as possible.

Readers Have Routines

Now that children are getting comfortable with how reading feels in your classroom, you can begin to establish the routines that help reading workshop become longer and more productive. Try asking children what they need in place to feel successful in reading workshop. You may have some of your own ideas in mind already, and asking children for input doesn't mean you have to give them up. It does communicate to children that their voices are valued in your room. They will probably say a lot of the things you would say anyway, but using different words. Feel free to add anything that matters to you if children don't suggest it. You are part of the community, too!

Keep in mind that you need to build up the routines and stamina gradually. Sometimes I ask the teachers I work with to list all of the things that children do that can be annoying in the first month of school. I hear things like, "When students say, 'I'm done' and we've only been reading for a few minutes" and "When I'm trying to confer and I have a trail of children behind me asking for help." The lists can be long. "Look at the bright side," I say, "All those things that bother you? That's two weeks worth of curriculum!" You see, children learn not to do the things that bother us because we *teach* them to do other things. Instead of saying, "I'm done," children can learn a few ways to stay productive during reading workshop. Instead of interrupting a conference, children can use some simple strategies for figuring out words or moving on to another book.

I try to remind myself that if I haven't taught something yet, it's unfair to expect students to know it. This keeps me from getting too discombobulated by the September chaos. It also helps me prioritize, because whatever bugs me most is what I have to teach first. The lessons I name in this section of the study are some of the most predictable ones I can think of, in an order that makes sense to me. You may need to add to these from your own list of things that bother you, and you may want to change the order based on your priorities.

The beginning of the year can be frustrating because you know you have so many great things to teach about reading, but you can't really teach them until your class is humming along, reading sort of quietly for about fifteen to twenty minutes. (Did I just say fifteen to twenty minutes? Relax. I'm hoping for this number by the end of the unit, or even by the end of the next unit.) In order to achieve this, you have to do a lot of reminding. Be a stickler! I interrupt reading workshop every time the noise goes over a certain level (I believe every teacher has an internal noise-o-meter that goes off when the noise crosses the line between productive and counterproductive). By the fourth interruption in a single day, children start to get the message that I am serious. I let them know that it is for their benefit and not because I am an ogre. "You told me you needed a quiet place to read, and I really want to give it to you, but I need your help! I will remind you as many times as it takes to give you the quiet room you asked for." Of course, this also has to be followed by a compliment at the end of the workshop. "Wow! Did you hear that? That last minute of reading workshop was so quiet. It wasn't silent because everyone was reading in a nice quiet voice. It was exactly the right amount of sound. It was the sound of first graders getting better at reading. How did it feel?" You get the idea.

Topics for Lessons, Conferences, or Mid-Workshop Focus Points

● *Readers treat their books with loving care.* Kindergartners do know how to treat books well, but something about those heady first days of first grade seems to make children a little frisky. We need to establish early on that books are not toys. They are certainly to be enjoyed and loved, but if they get ruined it should be because they were just read too much. This lesson also might include showing children how to browse for books in a basket, pull a couple out, carry them around, share them with a friend, and return them to the basket they came from.

● *Readers choose books they think they can spend some time with.* We might not have set children up with their book baggies yet, but we do want them to begin to choose books that they can stick with for a whole week. This could mean a book has cool pictures, fun characters, or a familiar story or is interesting in some other way. What we don't want students doing is randomly grabbing books and then randomly looking at them. From the very beginning, our expectation is that children engage with their books.

● *Readers move around the space quietly so as not to distract other readers.* This lesson has always been most successful for me when I actually demonstrated it. I show children how I get up from the meeting area, walk to my table to get my book baggie, go to my reading spot, and sit down. I often think aloud a little as I walk, anticipating the kinds of things that may go through children's heads so I can give them an alternate version: "Ooh, there's Ella! I really want to ask her to play with me at recess! No, no, I'll wait until later. Oh, but there are the book baskets! I could get some more books! No, I have great books already. I'll wait until Friday when we switch books." I also want to catch children in the act of walking around quietly so I can point it out to the class: "Hey, everyone, look how beautifully Kai is getting from his table to his reading spot. Wow, Kai, how do you do it?"

● *Readers find out as much as they can about their books before they start reading.* As children read different levels of books and different kinds of books, they need different strategies for getting their minds ready to read. Early in the year, I imagine children are reading simple pattern books. Show them how to think about the title and cover of a book, predicting what the whole book might be about. Also show them how you look at a few pages, thinking aloud about what words you might see when you do start reading.

A teacher I once worked with described this as *turning on the lightbulb*, and I thought this was perfect. Imagine going into a dark and unfamiliar room. If you reach in and turn on the light first, you can get the lay of the land before entering the room. You know where the window and the closet are now, where to go sit down and rest, where to put your bags down. What if the light wasn't working and all you had was a flashlight? You'd have to grope around, blindly feeling your way, stumbling and backtracking until you had a sense of the room. We want children reading books with the lights on, not with a little flashlight.

- *A book's repeated pattern can make it easier to read.* The earliest levels of books are designed to be accessible to children who are working on one-to-one matching, using pictures to help make meaning, and have just a few sight words. We need to teach students how to learn and remember the pattern so that they can put most of their mental energy into matching printed words with spoken words and figuring out the one or two words that change. We may need to give children the patterns of a lot of books. This is sort of like a jump start and in no way robs students of an opportunity to grow as readers. In fact, it may actually help them acquire more sight words.

- *Readers look at the words they're reading, even if they know them by heart (they may even point to each word with a finger).* Have you ever heard a child say, "I can read this whole book without even looking!" This is one outcome of teaching them to use a pattern. Now we need to teach them to point, cleanly and accurately, under each word exactly as they say it.

- *Readers get stronger by spending time with the same books.* This is not as much an explicit strategy lessons as it is an introduction to personal book baggies. Give children bags labeled with their names and tell them that today is a really great day because they are now moving into a more grown-up way of reading. Instead of choosing books from bins on the table, they are now ready to collect five (or six or seven) books for the whole week! What amazing good fortune has befallen your classroom!

I usually let children choose whatever they want for the first week. I want the baggies to feel like a new privilege and not something that's surrounded by rules. As I confer with children this week, I address the issue of *just-right books*, sometimes asking students to exchange some of their books for better choices. When it comes time to choose new books, I teach a whole-class lesson on the topic. I may introduce this by telling the class how a few children the prior week had made important decisions to exchange their books for ones they felt were a better fit. Nobody needs to know they did this with my encouragement.

● ***Sometimes it's good to read with a partner. To do this, move your chair or body to be sitting next to one another.*** You may not want to set up long-term partnerships this early in the year, but you can have children read with buddies in a more casual way. You'll teach a lot of reading skills that require strong partnerships. Before you can expect children to work, talk, and think well together, they need to learn the procedures of partnership. The simplest way to set this up is to have partners start sitting back to back for their private reading time. On your signal that it is time for partner reading time, they shift their bodies or chairs to now be sitting side by side.

● ***Readers sometimes have a special place to read.*** Though not essential, it can be nice to allow children to have special reading spots in the classroom. Some children read best at a table, while others may focus better in a quiet corner or lying on the floor. I actually find the management of reading workshop easier when children have reading spots all over the room. Not only are they in spots that match their learning preferences, but they are also more separate from one another and therefore less apt to get distracted by a classmate. If you do choose to give them spots, you might want to have them try out different places in the room over a couple of days, observing how they respond. Then you can assign semipermanent spots so that everyone knows where to go as soon as the lesson is over.

● ***One way to stay productive during reading workshop is to reread your book, trying to make it sound nice and smooth.*** Early in the year, children do not have a lot of stamina for reading. This comes in part from not knowing how to read very well, in part from having had two months away from school, and in part from not really knowing what to do in reading workshop besides, well, read. You can address the last of these reasons easily by giving children options for how to stay productive during their reading time. If a child gets tired of reading before the time is up, she can reread a book with an emphasis on making it sound smooth. This is far less taxing than decoding a brand-new book, and far more productive than saying, "I'm done!" or distracting her classmates.

● ***One way to stay productive in reading workshop is to find a page in your book you'd like to show your partner.*** In the spirit of the previous lesson, this one gives children a productive option for how to use reading workshop time, even if they do not feel equipped to start reading a brand-new book. Show them how you can go back through a book you have read, looking for a page you'd like to share with your partner. If you are feeling intrepid, you might even show children how to mark this page with a sticky note so they can remember it later, when you give the signal for partner time to begin.

● *If you get to a tough word in your book, see if the picture can help you.* When children are first able to decode, it must feel amazing to them. Suddenly the mystery of these squiggly marks on the page is becoming unlocked! A common response to this is for children to become so focused on the print that they forget about meaning, at least for a little while. I have seen children work so hard to sound out a word, when a strategically supportive picture was right in front of their eyes. Show children how when one strategy for figuring out words doesn't work, you look at the picture and think about what would make sense. This helps them be resourceful word solvers and, more important, it helps them keep a tight hold on meaning.

● *If someone near you is distracting you, give a gentle reminder of how reading workshop goes.* You have given children options for how to stay productive during reading workshop, and you have shown them how to move around the room quietly. It does take time for these behaviors to become habit, though. To remind children of the routines, enlist your budding community to help out. This lesson is great because it addresses two distinct groups in your class. It is certainly a reminder to the more distraction-prone children that you expect them to stay focused during the workshop, but it also addresses the children who are hard at work (and may love to let you know who is not). Let those children know that you appreciate their desire to keep reading workshop quiet and purposeful, and that the best way for them to help is gently and kindly to remind others to do the same. When I see this happen, I often comment on it: "Wow, you guys, I just saw the coolest thing. James was starting to get distracted and bouncing his chair up and down. Tyler so nicely and calmly reminded him of our chart of things to do in reading workshop. He wasn't bossy about it, he was just polite. Was that nice for you, James? Yeah, I know when I get distracted all I need is a gentle reminder to get back on track."

Creating a chart of ways readers can stay productive during reading time is helpful. It reminds students that there are options for how to use reading workshop time. Students can remind one another to look at the chart so that your time can be put to better use.

> ## Things to Do in Reading Workshop
>
> - Private Time
>   - Read a new book
>   - Reread a book
>   - Look through the pictures, imagining what the characters are saying
>   - Find two books in your baggy that go together and think about why
>   - Find a page you'd like to share with your partner
>   - Find what you think is the most important page, and think about why
> - Partner Time
>   - Read together
>   - Tell your partner what your whole book is about (not just a few pages)
>   - Swap books
>   - Act out a book together

Figure 1–2 Chart of Reading Habits

Reflecting and Celebrating

The community is coming along and your management feels pretty secure. Children know the routines and are getting comfortable with reading and with one another. It's time to honor this amazing accomplishment. Allowing and encouraging children to put into words how they feel about their progress helps them take ownership and therefore responsibility for learning. Stopping to celebrate along the way helps get students invested in keeping up the hard work.

Name__MURPHY__ Date_____

I am the kind of reader who...

Likes to read in this place

Likes to read this kind of book

Likes to read with these people

Figure 1–3 Murphy used pictures to tell me about himself as a reader.

Name Caroline   Date_____

I am the kind of reader who...

Likes to read in this place

I N the LIBRARY

Likes to read this kind of book

SeASAMe StReet

Likes to read with these people

BY MYSelf

Figure 1–4 Caroline wrote words to tell about herself as a reader.

STUDENTS' WORK SHOWS THAT I . . .	NEED TO TEACH OR RETEACH THIS TO THE WHOLE CLASS	NEED TO REMIND CHILDREN OF THIS SKILL	NEED TO TEACH THIS TO A SMALL GROUP OR IN A CONFERENCE	NEED TO CONGRATULATE CHILDREN FOR HOW WELL THEY DID IT
CHILDREN:				
Share favorite books with peers	☐	☐	☐	☐
Show engagement with reading material	☐	☐	☐	☐
Say what books are mostly about	☐	☐	☐	☐
Use pictures as a source of information while reading	☐	☐	☐	☐
Identify word wall words (words that have been taught separately) in their books	☐	☐	☐	☐
Choose books thoughtfully	☐	☐	☐	☐
Handle books carefully	☐	☐	☐	☐
Get to and from the meeting area quickly and quietly	☐	☐	☐	☐
Stay productive for about 15–20 minutes (by the end of the unit—this includes partner and private reading time)	☐			
Talk about their books	☐	☐	☐	☐
Discuss books with partners	☐	☐	☐	☐
Participate in lessons and discussions	☐	☐	☐	☐
Respect the range of abilities in the class	☐	☐	☐	☐
Treat other readers' time, ideas, and space with respect	☐	☐	☐	☐

Figure 1–5 Student Work Chart

Guiding Questions

● *How are we more grown up as readers now than we were on the first day of school?* Building a reading community means helping children feel a sense of ownership and agency in the classroom. Of course, I acknowledge their achievements, but it may carry more weight if I can help them recognize and celebrate their hard work. This is why I ask children to name the ways in which they feel more mature as readers than they did a mere few weeks before. Feeling good about these behaviors gives children the motivation to maintain a thriving community. I like to give children a sheet (see Appendix A-1) on which they can express, in drawing or writing, their identities as readers. We'll refer back to this at the end of the year.

● *What questions or compliments do you have for one another about your reading growth?* When a community has strong individual members, they are able to support and motivate one another. Rather than a competitive spirit, this kind of question encourages one of cooperation. Part of my goal here is for children to be proud of one another despite reading level.

■ Checking In

Now that you have laid the foundations of a strong community, you are ready to roll up your sleeves and dig into the meaty work of reading instruction. Without doubt, you will need to remind children of some of the lessons in this unit from time to time. That does not mean your community is failing, but just that you are all human beings. With a sense of shared responsibility and mutual caring, your students have what they need to take the risks necessary for success.

■ Professional Resources

Peterson, Ralph. 1992. *Life in a Crowded Place: Making a Learning Community*. Portsmouth, NH: Heinemann.

Supporting the Unit

Setting Up Read-Aloud Routines: Basic Etiquette

Although these routines are described as "basic," you'll find that moving students from imitating to adopting your model of basic etiquette will keep you busy for now.

- Children should direct their eyes and ears at the speaker.

- They should be able to repeat what a peer has said.

- They should speak loud enough for the whole class to hear.

- They should avoid interrupting one another.

Shared Reading: Make It Joyful Through Music

Shared reading in the first month of school should be, above all else, joyful! As a classroom teacher, I sang with my class every day. Unable to play an instrument and not that confident a singer, I chose a CD player as my accompaniment. Try this activity to make reading together truly a community event.

- Choose songs or poems that are fun to sing together.

- Every few weeks, choose a new song or poem and chart the words. Keep all the charts hanging together in a stack so children can sing them whenever they want to.

- At the end of the year, you can make each child a CD with all the songs and poems, and a book with all the words typed and illustrated by students.

Partnership: Routines

In time you will be able to set up long-term partnerships, teaching children how to talk and grow great ideas together. For now, you have to lay some groundwork. Show children early on that reading workshop has two parts: private time and partner time.

- Consider having children sit back to back for private time and side by side for partner time.

- Explain how partners hold books between them and how they take turns choosing which book to read together.

2

Making Sense of Those Little Black Marks

My mother loves to tell me about how I learned to read as I learned to talk. The youngest of five children who all knew how to read when I was born, and the daughter of a determined mother, I could read my own name and a few other words before I turned three. By the time I was five, I could decode most of the *Los Angeles Times*—emphasis on the word *decode*. Our neighbor, Mrs. Palmieri, thought it was the craziest thing she had ever seen, and she had me perform this feat for her skeptical friends. This was my party trick! What nobody ever asked me was, "So what is this about?" The emperor's lack of clothes would quickly have been discovered.

The part of the story my mother does not love so much is that at six I refused to read outside of what was absolutely required at school and did not read for pleasure for a couple of years. Decoding was a cool trick, but it lost its appeal pretty quickly. It's true that my primary teachers all referred to me as a *reader* because I could decode at such a high level. It was not until I got the hang of comprehension that I became what *I* call a *reader*.

This experience has given me a cautious approach to the teaching of decoding. A unit of study on decoding is vital at this time in first grade, but I think that print strategies have to be part of a balanced plan that recognizes the goal of teaching children to make meaning. As soon as a community has started to form, we must dig right into the work of translating print into meaning. While some children come to first grade reading comfortably, the vast majority is just at the brink. They know the alphabet and can spell some words but are lost when faced with an actual book, no matter how simple the text. In this unit, we give children lots of ways to turn those black squiggles on the page into words. We can't stop there, though. The words have to go together meaningfully and interact with children's own thoughts and experiences. Many teachers find decoding easier to teach and assess than comprehension. It is. If we stop here, though, we contribute to children's and parents' already too common confusion of decoding with reading.

We must teach a whole host of strategies for getting and making meaning. This includes decoding strategies that encourage children to use meaning as a source of information (rather than always using phonics) as well as strategies to slow down and notice their thoughts as they read. The more attention children pay to their thoughts, the more their reading becomes a satisfying dialogue between reader and text. This is the state where we can really teach children to dig into meatier comprehension work. Children's regular use of language is another largely untapped source of information for reading. Most native speakers of Standard English have a well-developed ear for how book language should sound, which can help them predict words as they read. Those children who are learning Standard English can learn to use syntax not to predict but to confirm. Of course, we must teach children about visual information—phonics. Children who already know how to use meaning and language structure as sources of information use phonics much more effectively than those who are taught only phonics or are taught phonics first. Putting these three together—making meaning, using language knowledge, and decoding—leads to well-rounded readers who decode *and* comprehend texts.

A small part of this unit also focuses on incorporating dramatic play into children's reading work, encouraging them to act out parts of books, pretend to be characters, or imagine dialogue for characters they see in their books.

■ Overview

Even though this unit is primarily about print work, we need to make sure to hold onto the connection to meaning. It is common for early readers to get so caught up in decoding that they forget to pay attention to what their books are about. Of course this is natural, and it's the reason we ask our students to reread their books. Still, children need to know that when it comes to reading, the act of making meaning is important. Our teaching must reflect this value.

The unit begins with an emphasis on using meaning as a source of information for reading. The strategies we teach in the first section of the study involve developing an understanding of the text, so children have this to fall back on when words get hard. The second section of the study is a short one that focuses on teaching children to use their own natural language structures as a source of information, so children learn the habit of making their reading sound like language should sound. This is hard for speakers of languages or dialects other than Standard English. These students will need a lot of explicit support in shared reading.

The third section of the study outlines strategies for using visual (mostly graphophonic) information. You will not see the phrase "sound it out" anywhere in this unit. The strategies here are more specific and more tailored to the book levels children are likely to be reading early in first grade. Hopefully, after being taught about using meaning and syntax as sources of information, children will use the visual information supported by strong comprehension.

Finally, the unit ends with a day or so of reflection and maybe even a small celebration. Congratulating ourselves for hard work and accomplishment is not just for writing workshop!

■ Goals/Outcomes

While we always want our students to be well-rounded readers, the emphasis of this unit is primarily on decoding. We must also attend to comprehension, of course, but our comprehension work here is framed as a means to the end of figuring out what the little black marks in our books are trying to tell us. We also continue our work with building good reading habits. Many of the community goals from the previous unit have carried over into this one and will continue to carry over through the year.

Making Meaning

We hope children will

- orient themselves to their books before reading

- show a literal understanding of texts by retelling or saying what books are mostly about

- think about what is happening or what they are learning in their books while they read (though this may not happen the first time reading a given book)

Decoding

We hope children will

- regularly and independently use pictures as a source of information while reading

- use visual/phonics cues where appropriate to figure out new words

- monitor their reading to see that it makes sense

- monitor their reading to see that it sounds right

- confirm their reading against the visual information as appropriate

- automatically read a growing repertoire of sight words

- use analogy as a means of figuring out new words that look like familiar words

Reading Habits

We hope children will

- choose books at an appropriate level, or have a good reason for choosing books above or below this level

- explore a variety of texts

- get started quickly during reading time

- have a few ways to be productive during reading time (for twenty to twenty-five minutes by the end of the unit)

- talk about their books

Community

We hope children will

- discuss books with partners

- participate in lessons and discussions

- respect the range of abilities in the class

- treat other readers' time, ideas, and space with respect

- work together to decode

- help one another learn or remember to use strategies to decode (rather than just telling one another words)

- share their learning processes and make helpful or encouraging questions or comments during share sessions

■ Getting Ready to Teach

As you prepare to teach this unit, think about your students and what they need. This information will help you choose what to teach to the whole class and how to plan for small-group instruction. Next, gather and prepare the materials you'll need to teach these lessons. In order to demonstrate the strategies in this unit, and indeed in most of this book, you will have to role-play being someone who reads like a first grader. Kathy Collins approached this by calling on a much earlier version of herself to help with lessons. Her students knew whether they were watching First Grade Kathy or Grown-Up Kathy. Whether or not you create an alter ego, it helps to let children know they are watching you handle text not as an adult reader, but as a reader just like them.

Considering Students

It is vital to have at least an informal assessment of your students' reading levels and habits going into this unit. Choose what to teach based on what your children are ready for, which is probably going to change from year to year. One year you may find yourself teaching children how to manage pointing to words with one-to-one correspondence, while the next year's class has mastered this.

In order to choose the best lessons for this unit, you should have an idea of what levels your students are reading independently. You may also want to gather some other information about them as readers, such as whether they monitor for meaning or sense, how they choose books to read, or how they talk about their books.

Preparing Demonstration Materials

For this unit, you need several big books that resemble the books children will be reading. If you have access to a document camera or an overhead projector, you will be able to use any book in your library. Choose some books ahead of time that allow you to teach the print strategies described later in this chapter. You will want to keep these out of the library for a little while so that children can try the strategy in a text they have not seen before. Look through the books, imagining how you will demonstrate using the strategy, explain it in a way children can follow, and think aloud about what you are doing. Think also about how you will ask children to try the strategy right there in the lesson. Perhaps you'll demonstrate on the first few pages and then ask children to try on the next couple of pages.

Some of these lessons may be made easier if you prepare the text in some way. For example, if you want children to look at the picture to figure out an unknown word, you may want to cover that word. If you want children to act out what they see in the pictures before attending to the print, you'll have to cover all the words. If you have these materials prepared and set aside ahead of time, you can do the lesson right when you need it. Sometimes we plan to do a particular lesson on Thursday, but then we notice something in our students that tells us to teach it today. It's good to be ready for that!

Choosing Texts to Help You Teach

The books you use for lessons and shared reading in this unit will depend on what you have available and on which publishers your school prefers. Rather than mentioning specific titles, I'll give some helpful guidelines for choosing appropriate texts. Because the unit focuses on print strategies, use books that are on similar levels to those of most of your students. This likely means levels A to E/F. Keep a stack of big books at these levels handy so you will be ready to demonstrate a variety of strategies as needed. It helps to go through your big books with a pack of sticky notes. Write down the strategies that can easily be taught with each book. This is not a substitute for thoughtful lesson planning, but it does get you ready to respond to children's needs as they arise.

Though you will continue to read aloud rich books at higher levels, make a point of reading aloud books at levels A to F also. Show children how to think and talk well about these books. Too many of us think of the earlier levels as a necessary hurdle to jump over on the way to real reading. This is a disservice to the students who need our help in making meaning right from the beginning of their reading lives. Choosing these books to read aloud and engaging students in purposeful talk about them will help children see that this *is* real reading.

■ Teaching

Using Meaning as a Source of Information

Children need a lot of effective strategies right from the beginning. It's hard to prioritize when you wish you could teach all of the strategies at once, just to get kids up and running. At this point in the year, I find myself tempted to focus on decoding to such a degree that meaning goes to the back burner. This is especially easy if you think of the earliest levels of books as having no real substance, as I definitely used to. I mean, how much meat can be dug out of "I like to run, I like to play"? We sell our children short if we think of level A and B books merely as an annoying hurdle children have to clear before they can really read. In this section of the study, we can teach children how to use the pictures, the words, and their own thoughts to construct meaning that's bigger and deeper than that of the words alone.

TIME FRAME	SECTION OF STUDY	WHAT CHILDREN DO	WHAT WE TEACH
5–7 days	Using meaning as a source of information	• Read books for meaning • Use what they know about their books and information in pictures to help them decode unfamiliar words • Think about character • Begin to monitor for meaning, making sure their reading makes sense	Topics for lessons, conferences, or mid-workshop focus points • Readers figure out as much as they can about a book before they read it. • It can help to look through a book and imagine what it might say before you read it. • Many books have word patterns on every page, which helps us read them. • Often pictures in books tell us what some of the words are. • One thing to try when you get to a new word is think, "What would make sense here?" • Sometimes the word pattern changes, so we have to look carefully at the picture and think about what's going on to figure out the new words. • When we read, it's always good to notice when things don't make sense. • As we read, we can also imagine what the characters in our books are thinking.
2–3 days	Using syntax as a source of information	• Use their knowledge of how Standard English sounds to help them read • Begin to monitor for sense, making sure their reading sounds right	Topics for lessons, conferences, or mid-workshop focus points • One thing to try when you get to a word you don't know is think, "What would sound right here?" • When we read, it's always good to notice when things don't sound right.

Figure 2–1 Unit at a Glance

ing thoughts or feelings for them. We then encourage them to go further by role-playing, participating in scenes or interviews from the point of view of a character. Finally, we show them how to use dramatization to better understand informational texts. The purpose of these strategies and behaviors is to introduce children to the feeling of what it is like to read deeply—to identify with characters, envision the setting, follow the action, and otherwise abandon themselves to the world of a book. These activities, then, are not an end in themselves, but a means to deepening engagement.

As we encourage children to role-play, we must remember to keep them tethered to the books or we run the risk of their play inhibiting, rather than enhancing, comprehension. This usually doesn't happen when children have ample opportunities to explore fantasies of their own invention, so I strongly recommend providing time and space for children to structure their own play in centers such as blocks and dress-up, or any other place where they can freely create dramatic narratives together. By *tethered to the books* I do not mean tethered to my interpretation of what the book means. I do mean connected to the meaning they are constructing from the text, even if that meaning may not match up with mine.

■ Goals/Outcomes

The focus of this unit is on deepening engagement and comprehension. In order to achieve this, I hope children will be able to breathe life into characters, unself-consciously talking and thinking as the characters might. Despite this emphasis, I also want to make sure to keep teaching decoding strategies as students read more demanding books.

Making Meaning

We hope children will

- orient themselves to their books before reading

- use dramatization as a way to engage with reading material

- describe the characters in their books

- show an understanding of characters' feelings, motivations, or experiences

- think about what their books are about after reading them

Decoding

We hope children will

- continue to use previously learned strategies with greater flexibility

- automatically read a growing repertoire of sight words

- blend parts of words, or chunks, to solve new words

Reading Habits

We hope children will

- remain productive during reading time (for thirty minutes by the end of the unit)

- occasionally act out books or parts of books

- read with appropriate expression

Community

We hope children will

- work with others to dramatize books or parts of books

- participate in lessons and discussions about dramatization

- share their learning processes and make helpful or encouraging questions or comments during share sessions

■ Getting Ready to Teach

Before you start this unit, read through the rest of the chapter with a pen and some sticky notes. This is a less common unit than some of the other ones in this book, and it makes sense to take notes ahead of time on ideas that seem new or unfamiliar. Doing this will make it easier to gather the materials you think you'll want to use to demonstrate as well as the books your children will have the most success in dramatizing.

Gathering Materials

This work was designed around the books I see children reading everywhere I go, so no special materials are required. The books you already have in your classroom library will work. While the lesson ideas refer to books with characters, I also suggest some lessons that address nonfiction. This means you can continue to encourage your students to choose a variety of books to keep in their baggies.

Considering Students

As a first grade teacher, you probably have a wide range of readers in your class. The work described in this unit looks different depending on who's doing it: Children reading very early levels might dramatize every page, while children in much higher levels will dramatize only certain scenes, and even then they'll do it silently. As you prepare to teach the unit, think about those students who read earlier or later levels than the majority. You'll want to plan some small-group lessons to show these children how dramatizing might look different in their levels. I encourage you to do this especially with the earliest readers. We tend to focus on decoding skills with this group as a kind of triage, forgetting that we still need to teach them the rich comprehension skills offered in this unit.

Preparing Demonstration Materials

You will coach children to try many of these strategies through whole-class read-aloud. It's a rich experience to role-play Sophie and Wendell sorting out their difficulties, or George and Martha talking through a misunderstanding. It can be hard for children to transfer these skills into their own reading, especially when they may be reading books far simpler than these. A key to the success of this unit is demonstrating many of the strategies in books like the ones children in the class are reading. It also helps to identify children who have a knack for portraying characters, and asking those students to help with the lessons. When children see peers acting out parts of their books, it suddenly becomes within reach.

Choosing Texts to Help You Teach

Choose books with strong characters and good dialogue for read-aloud, demonstrations, and shared reading. You might use books that most children cannot yet read independently:

- Ezra Jack Keats
  - *Peter's Chair*
  - *Goggles*
  - *Jennie's Hat*
  - *Pet Show!*

- Cynthia Rylant
  - Poppleton series
  - Henry and Mudge series

- Kevin Henkes
  - *Julius, Baby of the World*
  - *Lilly's Purple Plastic Purse*
  - *A Weekend with Wendell*

- David Shannon
  - *No, David!*
  - *David Gets in Trouble*
  - *David Goes to School*

It is also important to read aloud and demonstrate lesson topics with books that most children can access independently. Brand New Readers (small books from Candlewick Press) are great choices as well, and are written at the levels of many of your students. These books feature many fun characters, both animal and human. Don't forget to include nonfiction in read-aloud and in lessons.

◼ Teaching

Getting the Story into Your Body

The first section of this unit encourages children to get more personally involved in the stories they read. Even in books with strong picture support, visualizing the setting or the unfolding of events is a key component of comprehension. When we ask children to endow characters with thoughts or feelings, we lay the groundwork for making the kind of personal connections to books that enhance comprehension, rather than surface-level connections, which can actually get in the way of understanding.

Topics for Lessons, Conferences, or Mid-Workshop Focus Points

- *Imagine yourself in the setting.* Sometimes the setting of a book has a set of feelings or sensations associated with it. The park, the circus, the beach, Grandma's house, school, your own room, and so on—all of these places have some sort of meaning. This lesson asks children to consider this meaning briefly before they read the rest of the book, taking on any feelings that clearly go with the setting. Not all books will lend themselves equally to this, but when they do it can make a big difference with children's involvement in the story. If you

TIME FRAME	SECTION OF STUDY	WHAT CHILDREN DO	WHAT WE TEACH
4–5 days	Getting the story into your body	• Reread books or parts of books, acting them out in different ways: saying what characters might be thinking, role-playing a scene between two characters, or imagining a monologue for a character	Topics for lessons, conferences, or mid-workshop focus points • Imagine yourself in the setting. • After reading the words in the text, go back and imagine a character's thoughts. • After reading the text, go back and imagine the characters talking to one another.
5–7 days	Getting into the character's mind	• Investigate characters' inner lives by giving voice to their motivations, feelings, reactions, and observations about what is happening to or around them	Guiding question • Why do characters act the way they do? Topics for lessons, conferences, or mid-workshop focus points • Knowing characters better helps us understand stories better. Try answering questions as you read, from the point of view of a character: • "What are you thinking?" or "How are you feeling?" • "What makes you think that?" or "What makes you feel that way?" • "Why are you doing that?" or "Why did you do/say that?" • "What do you want?" • Acting out all or part of the book with a partner can help us both understand the story better.
4–5 days	Bringing information to life	• Practice dramatization strategies for understanding nonfiction texts	Topics for lessons, conferences, or mid-workshop focus points • Talking to a picture in a nonfiction book can help us understand what we are reading. • Gestures can help us visualize facts. • Gestures can help us visualize movement.
1 day	Celebration	• Act out books or scenes from books, using both the words from the text and their own inferred or interpreted words	

Figure 3–1 Unit at a Glance

have a copy of *In a Dark, Dark Wood* by Joy Cowley, for instance, try having children imagine themselves in a dark forest before reading. When they take on the cool, dark, damp, slightly ominous sensations of the setting, they read the book with much more suspense. Using an example as concrete as this helps them see the point of trying this exercise in other books.

● *After reading the words in the text, go back and imagine a character's thoughts.* In early levels of books, there aren't a lot of words telling the story. The picture does a lot of the work. If children don't spend any time looking at the picture, they miss out on a lot of story. Some books actually have a different,

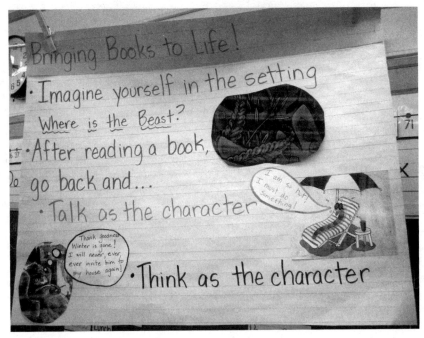

Figure 3–2 Bringing Books to Life

or at least richer, story happening in the pictures than what is suggested by the words. In this lesson, we ask children not just to look more closely at the picture, but to fill in details using their own imaginations.

In a highly patterned book, children might do this after every line or page: "'Mom is swimming.' Hey, come on in, sweetie, it feels nice. 'Mom is cleaning.' Could you help me with this? 'Mom is sleeping.' Boy, am I tired after all those things I did."

In a less patterned book, children could stop after every page or two of narrative to sum up a character's thoughts: "Phew. It's been a lot of work making this cake. I hope Mrs. Teaberry likes it!"

It's worth spending a couple of days on this topic early in the unit. You will probably have to remind children to continue to do this work throughout the unit, though they will begin to internalize it and do it silently later on.

● **After reading the text, go back and imagine the characters talking to one another.** In this lesson, children consider the points of view of more than one character. Many of the books they read have more than one main character, and we want them to be able to identify or empathize with both. As in the preceding lesson, ask children to read the text first, then to go back through the story, this time using the picture and what is in the text to create a bit of dialogue between the characters.

Getting into the Character's Mind

The first step in this unit was getting children to physically embody characters. You will now invite them into the characters' minds. In this section of the study, children will learn to ask questions of their characters and then to answer those questions from the characters' point of view. It's important to distinguish here between, "How does the character feel about the situation?" and "How would you feel in this situation?" You will probably have to make this distinction explicit for children, by thinking aloud about it every time you demonstrate a strategy.

Guiding Question

- *Why do characters act the way they do?* As I bring the class together on this day, it is not to teach a new strategy but to plant the seed of inquiry that will fuel the rest of the unit. I ask this question early in the unit not because we already have all the answers but so the class can keep it in mind as they read. If we believe that comprehension occurs not in the text or the reader, but in the space between them, we must teach children to ask questions and engage their thinking *before* they read.

It may help to create a chart here, to which we can refer children for the remainder of the unit, suggesting ways they can peek into their characters' minds (see Figure 3–3).

Topics for Lessons, Conferences, or Mid-Workshop Focus Points

- *Knowing characters better helps us understand stories better. Try answering questions as you read, from the point of view of a character.* As part of knowing their characters more deeply, encourage children to think specifically about what might be going on in the hearts and minds of the characters in their books. Over several days, guide them through asking characters questions and trying to answer the questions from the perspective of the character. The questions in Figure 3–1 are just suggestions or possibilities. They need not become a checklist that children have to complete every time they read, but rather a menu from which to pick and choose. You may want to provide children with sticky notes or bookmarks to record their thinking. They could jot or sketch an idea into a thought bubble if they're recording the character's thoughts, or a heart if they

Getting into our Characters' Minds

How would your character answer these questions?

- What are you thinking?

- How are you feeling?

- What makes you think that?

- What makes you feel that way?

- Why are you doing that?

- Why did you do or say that?

- What do you want?

Figure 3–3 Strategy Chart

are recording a character's feelings, for example. This will help them prepare for talking about their books with partners.

You can support this work in your read-aloud by asking children questions as if they are the characters. Instead of asking "Why do you think Peter is so upset about his chair being painted pink?" try asking "Peter, why are you so upset?" I encourage you to experiment with this way of talking to your class during read-aloud, noting the kinds of answers your students give. Recently when I read aloud *Peter's Chair* by Ezra Jack Keats, to a class, I asked both of the previous questions so the teachers and I could compare responses. The first question yielded responses like "He's mad" and "He's upset because he doesn't want Susie to have his chair." Responses to the second question included "I'm jealous" and "She's getting all my things!" Clearly casting the students in the role of the character helped them empathize with him and made their answers more insightful.

• *What are you thinking? How are you feeling?* This is essentially the question children asked characters in the whole first section of the study, and dramatizing was a way of giving the answer. When you add these questions to the repertoire, remind children that they have been doing this work all along. Encourage them to continue to dramatize as a way of identifying, naming, and sharing their characters' thoughts and feelings.

• *What makes you think that? What makes you feel that way?* This question can help children think about cause and effect in a concrete way, and it also helps children begin to give evidence for their thinking. Here's a scenario from a recent shared reading session I observed. The book was *Mr. Grump* by Joy Cowley, in which the title character growls grumpily at everyone. After Mrs. Grump kisses him, he turns unexpectedly pleasant. Here the teacher asked Mr. Grump about his thoughts and feelings:

TEACHER:	Mr. Grump, how are you feeling?
AARON:	I'm grumpy. I'm *always* grumpy!
TEACHER:	Why are you being so grumpy to the mail carrier?
JULIA:	Because it's all just bills!

Later in the same session:

TEACHER:	Mr. Grump, you seem to be feeling better. Are you?
SYLVIE:	Yes, I'm much happier now.
ANTONIO:	Yeah, I felt better when Mrs. Grump kissed me.
TEACHER:	What about you, Mail Carrier? You seem surprised.
CYRIL:	Mr. Grump is always grumpy. This just doesn't make any sense.

Even if it seems like too much to ask children to do this independently, try supporting them to think this way in shared reading sessions or during a read-aloud. You will be amazed at their thinking! I always am.

• *Why are you doing that? Why did you do/say that?* Imagining a character's motivations for behaving a certain way helps give life to that character. In doing this, children consider more carefully characters' traits and how these might influence characters' behavior as they respond to what is happening in the plot. What is Biscuit really doing when he keeps getting out of his bed? What is Huggles really doing when he keeps trying to hug all the zoo animals? Just asking this question, even if the answer doesn't immediately come to mind, requires thinking about the character on a deeper level.

• *What do you want?* I love this question. Or, more accurately, I love to watch children grapple with this question. What a character wants is seldom laid out explicitly for the reader. Part of the fun of reading is trying to figure out what characters want. The ways that children suggest and discuss how characters might answer this question say a lot about how they understand their books. Perhaps what I love most about this question is that it helps children do sophisticated comprehension work regardless of their reading level.

• *Acting out all or part of the book with a partner can help us both understand the story better.* This can be an item on the menu of activities for partners to choose from during reading workshop, or it can be a center activity that children can choose. Either way, children work together to act out whole books, if the books are relatively short, or scenes from longer books. Children work together to figure out how to act out the book: who plays what part, will they need simple props, which scene will work best, and so on. After making some of these choices, they should have the book sitting nearby, ready to consult if they need to be reminded of what happens. You will probably need to demonstrate this with another adult or with a child whom you've prepared for the occasion. If two children in the class have done this successfully, ask them to demonstrate and explain for the class how they were able to work well together.

Bringing Information to Life

This final section of the study shifts gears dramatically. The unit until now has focused on fiction, but many children probably have nonfiction texts in their baggies, too. Rather than ignoring these books for the whole unit, take a few days to show children how they can also use dramatization to better understand nonfiction books. Rather than acting out what characters say, think, feel, or do, children use gesture to act out information. This will help them visualize what they are learning. Two of these lessons will reappear in the nonfiction unit, but in a more advanced form.

Topics for Lessons, Conferences, or Mid-Workshop Focus Points

• *Talking to a picture in a nonfiction book can help us understand what we are reading.* Here, instead of talking *from* the point of view of what they see in the picture, ask children to talk *to* the picture. They can narrate what they see or ask questions about it. Children are probably reading earlier levels of nonfiction books at this point in the year, which might not have that many words on a page. Talking to the pictures helps students spend more time looking at the pictures, instead of just reading the one or two sentences and flipping to the next page.

- *Gestures can help us visualize facts.* A lot of the earlier nonfiction books have just a little bit of text to go along with a photograph. It can be enough just to study and talk about (or to) the picture, but sometimes it helps make information more concrete to create a gesture to go with it. Stopping to act out having arms as big as your whole body, as the praying mantis does, or having ankles halfway up your leg, as a flamingo does, doesn't take that much time away from their reading but adds a lot to children's understanding.

- *Gestures can help us visualize movement.* As you demonstrate this one, think aloud about how you might create an image in your mind that moves or is different from the one in the picture in some way. Show children how to use hand gestures or sketches to support creating an image: "It says the snake slithers. I can make my hand move just like a snake. This is what slithering is! Here it says the snake squeezes its food. I can do that with my hands, too." Facts become not just words to repeat, but images, which become schema, which become a more and more complete vision of the world around them.

Celebrating

It scarcely needs to be said, but a great way to celebrate this unit is to invite children to perform favorite books or scenes for the class (or for families or guests if you like). Children can do this individually or in partners, depending on the books. You may want to let children create simple costumes or props to go with their performances, but it's not essential.

■ Checking In

This unit segues nicely into the one that follows, "Reading with a Wide-Awake Mind." In the next unit, we focus on the internal thinking children do as they read, broadening their repertoire of ways to think as they read. Just because this unit is over doesn't mean children are ready to stop doing this work, though. Think about keeping some of the dramatization work alive in center time or partner time in the months to come.

STUDENTS' WORK SHOWS THAT I . . .	NEED TO TEACH OR RETEACH THIS TO THE WHOLE CLASS	NEED TO REMIND CHILDREN OF THIS SKILL	NEED TO TEACH THIS TO A SMALL GROUP OR IN A CONFERENCE	NEED TO CONGRATULATE CHILDREN FOR HOW WELL THEY DID IT
CHILDREN:				
Orient themselves to their books before reading	☐	☐	☐	☐
Use dramatization as a way to engage with reading material	☐	☐	☐	☐
Describe the characters in their books	☐ ☐	☐ ☐	☐ ☐	☐ ☐
Show an understanding of characters' feelings, motivations, or experiences	☐	☐	☐	☐
Think about what their books are about after reading them	☐	☐	☐	☐
Continue to use previously learned strategies with greater flexibility	☐	☐	☐	☐
Automatically read a growing repertoire of sight words	☐ ☐	☐ ☐	☐ ☐	☐ ☐
Blend parts of words, or chunks, to solve new words	☐ ☐	☐	☐ ☐	☐ ☐
Remain productive during reading time (for thirty minutes by the end of the unit)	☐ ☐	☐ ☐	☐ ☐	☐ ☐
Occasionally act out books or parts of books	☐	☐	☐	☐ ☐
Read with appropriate expression	☐ ☐	☐	☐ ☐	☐
Work with others to dramatize books or parts of books	☐	☐	☐	☐
Discuss books with partners	☐	☐	☐	☐
Participate in lessons and discussions about dramatization	☐	☐	☐	☐
Share their learning processes and make helpful or encouraging questions or comments during share sessions	☐	☐	☐	☐

Figure 3–4 Student Work Chart

Supporting the Unit

Read Aloud with Purposeful Talk

If your students are getting better at sticking to one or two topics during whole-class conversations about books, begin to teach them ways to extend another's ideas.

- Children can ask questions to clarify what they hear ("What do you mean?" or "What makes you think that?").

- Children can agree or disagree, giving evidence from the text ("I don't think so because _____." Or "I thought the same thing because _____.").

- Children can suggest ideas they are not sure about, to see what the group thinks ("I'm not sure, but I think that maybe _____. Was anybody else thinking about that?").

It is also important to continue to support the work of dramatization through the read-aloud.

- At key points in some of your books, address the class as a character from the book, inviting students to respond as the character ("Why do you feel that way?" or "Why did you do that?").

Shared Reading: Practicing Print Strategies

In this unit continue to practice print strategies in the highly supported context of shared reading. Of course, your joyful songs and poems will continue. Use most of your shared reading time to give children opportunities to "become" the characters in their favorite books.

- Continue to choose songs or poems that are fun to sing together.

- Choose some big books that have strong or interesting characters. Invite children to embody these characters, choosing more than one character from a book ("Everybody be Mr. Grump. Ooooh, grumpy! OK, now be the mail carrier.").

- As in the read-aloud, address children as if they were the characters. Ask them about their feelings and motivations.

Partnership: Drama

- Partners in this unit can work together to bring their books to life and to talk about their thinking.

- Partners can act out a book together, taking turns choosing the book.

- Partners can talk about why the characters are acting as they are.

- Partners can take turns saying which page or part they thought was most important.

Working with More Advanced Readers

While it will be appropriate for most children to act out whole books, this doesn't make sense for anyone reading above about level F or G. As books get longer and more complex, the words do more work and the pictures do less. Acting out whole books will slow down children without supplying a lot of information that isn't in the words. If you have children reading above these levels, teach them how to stop and act out key parts.

- Act out parts where you think the character(s) might be having a strong feeling.

- Act out parts where characters are talking to one another, especially if they are arguing, fighting, making plans, feeling excited, or if you think it's important for any reason.

- Keep reading dialog with appropriate expression.

Children reading higher-level books are also being exposed to more sophisticated stories. You will need to teach them some ways to talk about their books with one another, taking into account the complexities of their books. These questions might not apply to the books most of the class are reading, but will certainly work in a small-group setting.

- One way to a talk about a book is to describe a character's journey.

- One way to talk about a book is to describe what changes.

- One way to talk about a book is to imagine what the author wants us to learn.

Working with Readers Who are Having a Hard Time

Children who have a hard time dramatizing their books may not be the same children who struggle with reading generally. You may, in fact, have some very advanced readers who have difficulty with this. Since the goal of this work isn't the drama but is the deepened connection to the characters and their stories that dramatization supports, you may be able to forge that connection through different avenues:

• More advanced decoders can stop to visualize parts of the text, and can jot or sketch what characters might be thinking or feeling.

• It can help to set up drama baskets, containing familiar favorite books and a few simple props, which children can use during center time or choice time to act out a story. If it feels more like a center and less like an academic activity, children may be more willing to take risks with it. Strategically grouping the reluctant actors with more willing students is helpful.

4

Reading with a Wide-Awake Mind

I don't know if this ever happens to you, but every now and then I look at the children I teach and think, "They have it so much better than I did!" I don't want to knock my childhood teachers (except maybe Mrs. Wallace, who clearly didn't like me very much) but I was raised on basal readers, which, in the seventies, were not known for their literary quality. I was taught to read in such a way that I could answer a predictable set of questions:

- What happened after _____? (Checking my literal comprehension)

- The character most likely felt _____. (Checking my basic inferring skills)

- It can be inferred that the author thinks a, b, c, or d? (Perhaps checking my mind-reading skills?)

These questions were coconspirators in a game of "right answer/wrong answer," something that has little to do with real reading. The passages themselves were written in such a way that there was no debate as to the correct answers to the questions, as there might be in a piece of actual literature.

And then there was *reading*. That thing I did at home, with books bought at the bookstore or borrowed from the library. This was entirely different from the reading I did in school, to the point where I didn't even think of them as the same activity. I could sit for hours in the same place, barely aware of the patch of sunshine traveling across the wall, past the armchair, and finally disappearing into a corner. Only then would I reluctantly put down my book to go set the table for dinner. If I was particularly enjoying a book, I would read the last few chapters slowly, backing up and rereading sections, stopping to think about the characters with whom I had become so entwined. It was always with a mixture of satisfaction and regret that I would close the book for the last time. Certain books are just too hard to say good-bye to.

It is not just a wide-awake mind but also a wide-open heart that I bring to my reading. My ability to decode words just opens the door, but the real reading happens when I step through. The magic is not in the book, no matter how good a book it is, and it is not in my head. The magic of reading happens somewhere between these two places, and feels to me like a current flowing in both directions. The thoughts, experiences, feelings, responses, and ideas that I bring to what I read are just as important as what is inside the book. Which means that each of us has an individual experience of reading any given book. Sure, we should all come away with the same literal understanding and basic inferences, but how we arrive at those—how we visualize the action or identify with a character's emotional state—is different for all of us. This unit is not about right answers. It's not really even about answers at all. It is about awakening the mind to the process of reading, and listening to everything that happens between the reader and the book.

■ Overview

The content of this unit is more abstract that that of the other units in this book, both for teachers and children. We just can't see comprehension happening, making it hard both to demonstrate and to assess. One way to make this work more concrete for children is to name and chart ways of thinking with students, using their own words as much as possible. Another way to support children who have a hard time with the metacognitive aspect of this work is to point out to the class whenever you see children thinking about their books in a way you have discussed: "Hey, can I stop you all for a minute? Jonathan is doing some interesting thinking. He said that the character in his book seems bossy and he wondered if it's going to turn out like *The Recess Queen* by Alexis

O'Neill and Laura Huliska-Beith. Remember what happened in that book? Jonathan was making a connection to another book. I'll bet a lot of you are thinking like that." When you give a specific example of a behavior, children better understand the concept.

The unit starts by calling attention to the ways children may already be aware of thinking as they read. The next section of the study suggests new ways children can activate their minds as they read, methods for noticing and keeping track of their thinking, and ways to then share this thinking with partners. As in all the units, I have included more teaching ideas in this section than you will need. What's different here is how many more. I can envision this unit going in many wonderful directions, depending on several factors. Your and your students' personalities and preferences, their reading levels, and their past experience with this kind of comprehension work will determine which lessons you teach and how much time you spend on each one. Let your assessments and instincts guide you. The study ends with a brief reflection and celebration.

■ Goals/Outcomes

The goals of this unit center on children becoming more aware of their mental activity as they read. This touches on the categories of making meaning and reading habits. Because of the social nature of the unit, we're also looking for growth in the reading community. Of course, we need to pay attention to decoding as well so that children can continue to cope with increasingly challenging books.

Making Meaning

We hope children will

- continue to dramatize books or parts of books

- maintain literal comprehension

- think while they read about any of the following things that are appropriate:
  - what is happening in the book
  - what they are learning
  - their prior knowledge
  - their questions
  - their predictions
  - what the book reminds them of

- infer where necessary

- have and share opinions about their books

- begin to monitor their comprehension

Decoding

We hope children will

- use decoding strategies with greater flexibility

Partnership

We hope children will

- discuss their thoughts with partners

- prepare for partner talk by using tools to keep track of their thinking

- read their partners' books

- talk and think together about books both partners have read

Reading Habits

We hope children will

- keep track of their thinking

- talk about books after reading them

Community

We hope children will

- participate in class conversations about books

- share their learning processes and make helpful or encouraging questions or comments during share sessions

■ Getting Ready to Teach

Before launching this unit, I recommend reading through the Teaching section to get familiar with the structure and content of the unit. You'll also want to think about which materials will work best for you and how you'll organize them. Imagine how your students might respond to this teaching and how your classroom library will support them. Finally, plan ahead how you'll demonstrate the concepts. Some of the ideas are a little abstract, but with a clean and clear demonstration you can make them accessible to your young learners.

Gathering Materials

This unit generally falls in December or January and can be accompanied by a growth spurt among your readers. If you held back any books from your library at the beginning of the year, now is a good time to introduce them. If you do not count yourself among the teachers who have a surplus of books, even the introduction of a couple of new books or series can light a new spark of excitement around your reading workshop. Aside from books, you'll need some sort of tool on which children can record their thinking as they read. The simplest of these is sticky notes, but you may prefer a nonsticky alternative, such as bookmarks made of cardstock or index cards cut in half. I do not recommend journals just yet. When children are new to tracking how they think as they read, they need to have the record of their thinking as close as possible to where that thinking happened—in this case, in the book.

Considering Students

This unit may not coincide with a full implementation of your formal assessment program, but it does merit a quick check in the form of an informal running record. It is important that children read books that are just right for them as they practice the thoughtful and purposeful comprehension work of this unit.

Preparing Demonstration Materials

As a primary teacher, you are no stranger to making complex or abstract ideas accessible to children who function more comfortably in the realm of the concrete. This unit will test that very strength. As you read ahead through the teaching ideas, make a note of which ones you will definitely want to demonstrate to your whole class. Get your hands on some books, preferably at a variety of reading levels, that will best help you illustrate the concepts you wish to teach. Use my sample dialogues to help you come up with ideas. Now find the exact page you want to use and mark it. The more specifically you plan in advance, the clearer the concept will be to your class. In some cases, you'll want to read aloud the whole book sometime before using it in a lesson, so plan for this, too. Don't forget to support this work through shared reading! Some of your favorite big books are wonderful invitations to think big thoughts.

Choosing Texts to Help You Teach

Return to many of the same books you used in the previous unit, again at a variety of levels. This will help you demonstrate explicitly the connection between dramatization and thinking about books. As you read a book again in the unit, you might think aloud about this:

"I remember when I acted this part out, how I thought Peter was angry, but also a little jealous. Now I'm not acting out the book, but I'm still thinking about how he feels."

Choose a couple of rich chapter books to read aloud during this unit. Children who are starting to read at higher levels, including chapter books, will need a lot of support in thinking about their books, now that a single book may take several sessions of reading to finish. Be sure to demonstrate some of these lessons with nonfiction as well as fiction!

■ Teaching

Exploring How We Think While We Read

At the beginning of the study, spend just a couple of days exploring the idea of thinking while reading. Many new readers approach reading as a one-way street—information flows from the book to the reader. Explain to them that, in fact, they are active and important participants in the process. In this section of the study, you may also want to start a cumulative chart, which will grow as the unit progresses, of ways that students are thinking as they read. Try to use your students' own language on the chart, as this will make it more accessible to those children for whom the concept is still a bit murky. Instead of writing "Readers infer," for example, you might write "Readers think about how characters might be feeling" or "Readers think about what an author might be trying to tell them."

Topics for Lessons, Conferences, or Mid-Workshop Focus Points

● *Readers think as they read.* This is a call to action and then, later, becomes a reminder. This lesson introduces a larger concept, and all the lessons that follow fit inside that concept. I can even see a chart in my mind's eye, with "Thinking While We Read" as the title, with many of the lessons that follow

TIME FRAME	SECTION OF STUDY	WHAT CHILDREN DO	WHAT WE TEACH
3–5 days	Exploring how we think while we read	• Pay attention to their mental activity as they read • Participate in whole-class and partner discussions about this	Guiding questions • How do we know we understand what we read? • What kinds of thinking do we do as we read?
10–15 days	Thinking more deeply as we read	• Continue reading appropriate books and talking about them with partners • Pay more attention to the thinking they do as they read • Try new kinds of thinking as they read • Grow partner talk	Topics for lessons, conferences, or mid-workshop focus points • Readers pay attention to what's happening in their books. • Readers use tools to help keep track of their thinking. • Readers notice when a book reminds them of something. • Our connections need to help us understand the books better. • Readers notice when they're thinking about something else. • The pictures in our books might tell us something more or different than what is in the words. • We can almost see the story happening when we imagine the pictures moving. • Readers give life to the characters they read about to better understand them. • Readers notice when they have questions. • Readers reread when something doesn't make sense. They may need to try some strategies to fix the problem. • Readers reread to make the book sound better or smoother. • Readers reread when they want to think more about something in the book. • Readers notice when the book gives them a strong feeling. • *Because* is an important word to use when we share our thinking. • Thinking about the most important part can help us understand the book. • Partners can use their notes to help start a conversation. • Partners can host a visit to one another's books.
1 day	Reflecting and celebrating	• Think and talk or write about what they have learned • Acknowledge and celebrate their progress	Guiding questions • How are we more grown up as readers now than we were a month ago? • If a new student came into our class and asked, "What is reading?" what would you say?

Figure 4–1 Unit at a Glance

underneath. Given the great importance this idea plays in the unit, make a big deal of it when you bring your class together to the meeting area:

> Friends, today is a big day. I have noticed that you are really growing up as readers. I think you are ready for me to teach you about a whole bunch of things readers do. You see, when readers really pay attention to what's happening in their books, a lot of things start happening in their own heads. I want to help you notice, keep track of, and talk about all the many thoughts that happen in your brain while you read. What you need to do from now on is turn your mind on so you can listen to everything that's happening in there. We're going to talk about a lot of ways to think while you read.

Of course many of your students already think as they read. It would be pretty hard not to. You will now teach them to listen to the thoughts they have and talk about them with the class or with a partner. As the unit goes on and the students name the various ways readers do this, the children will become more aware of their thoughts and will have a greater variety of kinds of thought.

Guiding Question

● *What kinds of thinking do we do as we read?* Another way to launch the unit is to present children with a question that will guide our conversation for the next few weeks. I ask this question first because I want to know how children will put their ideas into words, and second, as a frame for the whole study. You may want to chart all of the ways of thinking children do while they read throughout the course of the unit. This will help children become conscious of their thoughts as well as suggest new ways of thinking. One way to set this up is to point out some kinds of thinking you have noticed children doing with their sticky notes, and start the conversation by mentioning them: "At the end of the last unit people were putting a lot of stickies into their books. I want to share some of them with you. Anna wrote what she thought the character was thinking. She was getting in the character's head. Wyatt wrote that Biscuit was kind of like his brother. His book *reminded* him of something. I'm going to put these on our chart. The rest of the chart is blank. We'll be filling in all these other stickies as we keep discovering new ways to think while we read."

Thinking More Deeply as We Read

You have established that readers think while they read and that children will study how to do this. In this section of the study, help your students discover

Figure 4–2 At the beginning of the unit, show just one or two ways children might use sticky notes in their reading. Demonstrate how to use other notes as the unit goes on.

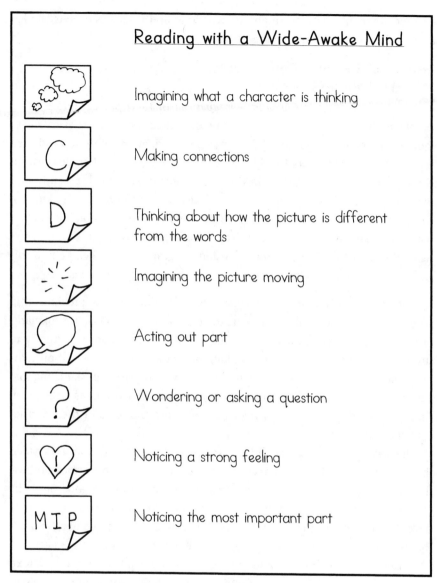

Figure 4–3 Later in the unit, your chart of sticky notes will be full.

a wider variety of thoughts, responses, reactions, and strategies readers employ as part of fully understanding their books.

Topics for Lessons, Conferences, or Mid-Workshop Focus Points

- *Readers pay attention to what's happening in their books.* Before going deeply into the unit, I want make it abundantly clear that I expect everyone to monitor their comprehension. In order to do any richer or more sophisticated thinking work in their books, children have to have a strong handle on what is happening at the literal level. My friend, Ginny Lockwood, recently told me, "People knock literal comprehension like it's less valid than other kinds of comprehension. It's not! You *have* to understand texts on a literal level before you can do any of the more sophisticated reading work we talk about." She's right. We can't take literal comprehension for granted. The idea behind this lesson is for children to keep a tight hold on the story as it unfolds.

- *Readers use tools to help keep track of their thinking.* In the previous unit, you might have asked children to write their character's thoughts on bookmarks or sticky notes. If you chose to do that, use this lesson as an opportunity to suggest recording other kinds of thinking. If you decided to hold off on written response, take a minute to reconsider it now. Any jotting or sketching that children do in their reading will help them notice their thoughts right when they have them, and they can refer back to those thoughts in their partner conversations.

  One way both to remind children to notice their thoughts and to widen the variety of thoughts they have is to provide tools for keeping track of those thoughts. Any tool that works for you and your students is a good one. The important thing is that children notice and jot or sketch a thought when they have it. Later, when they meet with their partners, they can go back and use the tool to facilitate their conversation. Some of the tools I have seen are:

  - Bookmarks with icons representing different possible responses to a text, such as a question mark to represent wondering something or a heart to represent having a strong feeling. These are copied onto cardstock. I have seen some teachers keep these in a central location, while others put them into a baggie for each student. As children read, they may leave bookmarks in their books as a record of thinking in a certain way. If you do something like this, be sure to give out blank bookmarks, too. These invite children to think in ways not yet taught, named, or imagined.

  - That old stand-by, the sticky note. (Before all the sticky note haters skip this part and move on to the next point, give me a minute. The benefits to

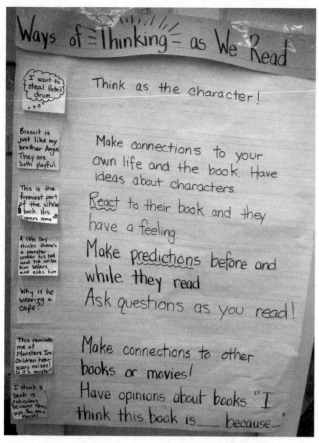

Figure 4–4 Using Sticky Notes to Think as We Read

children's comprehension of being able to notice, track, and discuss their thoughts vastly outweighs the pain-in-the-neck-ness of having stray sticky notes show up in a book long after the reader has moved on. A little bit of teaching into "leave a place cleaner than you found it" will help.) OK, back to sticky notes. You can teach children to jot words or use icons like those mentioned above onto notes. As children meet with their partners to discuss their thoughts, they can remove the notes from the book. As part of these lessons, you can make a chart of all the icons and what they mean. As I said earlier, invite and encourage children to use blank notes for ideas that may not fit so easily into an icon or a couple of words.

● ***Readers notice when a book reminds them of something.*** An active mind makes connections. When I introduce this concept to children, I don't specify what kinds of connections readers make (text to self, text to text, etc.). I just want them to be aware of it when their books stimulate a memory from their own lives or from another book. A lot of young readers make these connections naturally, but don't pay them too much mind. When children become aware that these connections are important, we can teach them how to use the connections to deepen comprehension. I might ask students to use a bookmark or sticky note when they are reminded of something, so they can bring this to their partner conversation.

Of course, if you feel compelled to teach about specific kinds of connections readers make, be sure to accompany this with lessons about using these specific kinds of connections to better engage with or understand the book, as in the following lesson.

- *Our connections need to help us understand the books better.* I've heard a lot of children proclaim with pride, "I made a connection!" and then turn the page without another word. Yes, awareness is the first step, but once they have that, we need to take it a bit further. If children are making connections just to say that they have something in common with a character, this is form without function. When I watch a child flip through pages saying, "My grandma makes cookies, too! My grandma plays with me, too!" I do not see connections being made. I see perhaps another level of retelling, but that's about it. In order for this to support comprehension, we have to use our common experience to understand, or even empathize with, the character. As you demonstrate this for children, show first the shallow connection that doesn't do much in the way of deepening comprehension: "My grandma makes cookies, too! My grandma plays with me, too!" Then think aloud about how you can take this thing you have in common with the character and use it to understand or empathize: "My grandma makes cookies and plays with me, too. I bet this character's grandma's house smells so good and is such a warm and comfortable and place to be. Maybe he just feels so safe and cared for when he goes there, like I did at my grandma's house. I'm going to keep that idea in my mind as I read on."

- *Readers notice when they're thinking about something else.* Let's face it. This happens to all of us more than we'd like. So we're truly teaching students a life skill when we teach them to notice this and bring themselves back to the book. I usually teach this lesson by striking up a friendly conversation between readers: "Hey, do you ever find yourself thinking about other things while you're reading? I mean, things that aren't the book? Sometimes when I'm reading I realize all of a sudden that I've been thinking about my friends or what I'm going to do during recess. Does that ever happen to you? Well, let me tell you a good way to take care of it when that happens."

Show children how to back up and reread a page or two, paying attention to the parts that got ignored the first time through. The point of this lesson is to notice when their attention has strayed. Once they do this, they can get themselves back on track.

- ***The pictures in our books might tell us something more or different than what is in the words.*** Especially at the earliest levels, but even in those chapter books that have illustrations, pictures often add to the words and sometimes even contradict them. Children's books have illustrations for a reason: to help readers make meaning. Teach children to read the pictures as carefully as they read the words. Model this when you read aloud, encourage it in shared reading, and demonstrate it explicitly in a lesson. It might sound like this: "Sometimes I feel like rushing through my books by looking only at the words. When I do that, I'm only getting some of the story, not all of it. I want to show you how careful readers read the words *and* the pictures. Watch me. This page says, 'Rusty helps me make my bed.' I could just turn the page and think that Rusty is helping the little girl make her bed. But look at the picture! Rusty, this dog, is pulling the covers *off* of the bed! That's not helping! Hmm. She must be joking. Let's see what happens next." This example is of a book in which the pictures and words do not match, but it's just as important when they do match: "It says, 'Big rabbit jumps. Little rabbit jumps, too.' I could turn the page without really looking at the picture, but that would only be getting part of the story. I'm going to look more closely at the picture. Oh, look at little rabbit! He couldn't jump over the fence so he jumped under it! The words said they both jumped, and they did both jump. The picture tells me they jumped in different ways, though! Wow, it's a good thing I stopped to look carefully! Do you see what I could've missed? Phew."

- ***We can almost see the story happening when we imagine the pictures moving.*** I suspect that we primary teachers don't see the need to teach a lot about visualization because children's books still have so many pictures. We don't want to leave them high and dry as their books start having less and less picture support, though. Most of the work of the previous unit provides a foundation for visualizing later. This lesson makes is a bit more explicit. While children's books still do have strong picture support, teach them to look at the pictures after they read the text, practically seeing the action unfold before their eyes:

> As I'm reading this book, I keep noticing Biscuit doing different things to keep from having to go to bed. If I stop to imagine this picture moving, I see Biscuit running around, back and forth, and maybe even jumping

a little bit. I see him acting like he wants to play. Oh, but here I see him finally climbing into the little basket. I bet he even yawned! When I do this it makes me feel like I know Biscuit a little better—like he's a real puppy and not just a character in a book.

● **Readers give life to the characters they read about to better understand them.** This lesson reaches back into the previous unit and connects dramatization to the thinking work of this unit. Remind children to act out what their characters might be thinking or saying. Show them how to mark a spot with a bookmark or sticky note where they felt particularly connected to the character. They should then bring this tool to their partner conversation so they can talk about this connection. This might sound like, "I put my sticky note here because this is the part where Little Chimp started climbing the tree. I thought his mama might be saying, 'I'll hold you in my arms.' I think Little Chimp was afraid but he climbed up anyway because his mama was there."

● **Readers notice when they have questions.** I sometimes have this odd experience in which I remember my mother in some situation or other as a bona fide grown-up who knew everything. Then I realize she was younger in the memory than I am now, and that she must have felt just as unsure or confused as I sometimes do. I wonder if children see reading as something adults do with perfection and confidence, and not as something we do with questions and wonder. This lesson is a nice opportunity to give children a glimpse of your own reading experience as something a bit uncertain:

> You know, when I first read this I thought Piggy just didn't realize she had thrown the ball all wrong and it landed behind her. I thought she really believed she had thrown the ball all the way around the world. Now as I think again, I wonder if she knows she can't throw very well. I wonder if it doesn't matter to her how well she throws like it matters to Gerald. And I wonder why she wouldn't just say so. I'm going to put a sticky note here with a question mark because I really, really want to talk more about this with my partner later.

● **Readers reread when something doesn't make sense. They may need to try some strategies to fix the problem.** Sometimes rereading alone helps children figure out and fix the problem: "'I went down the slid.' I mean, 'I went down the *slide.*'"

Other times, children will actually have to take a moment to decode a word or realize that they misread a word or skipped a line because the text is not consistently placed from page to page. Whatever the problem, fixing it usually starts with backing up and rereading. Trouble is harder to fix when we don't see it coming, as children don't when they are reading a text for the first time. If they reread, they know when the trouble is coming and can prepare for it by paying extra attention to what is going on there. Sometimes I demonstrate this in a read-aloud book, so children can't see the words and help me read them accurately. I'll show them how I read along and suddenly say a word that doesn't make sense: "'And then she went into the chairs.' Wait a minute, *chairs*? OK, I'm going to back up and reread this part. It's going to be something she can go into, and here in the picture is a house. Hmm. Look at this! This book has words above *and* below the picture. I was just looking down here! OK, here goes. 'And then she went into the house. She saw three chairs.' Aah, much better. So you see when I back up and reread, I don't just reread, but I also think about what would make sense in that spot."

- *Readers reread to make the book sound better or smoother.* Imagine children have a little energy meter that tells you what their brains are doing as they read. The first time they read a book (up to a point near level F or G), the meter will tell you that about 90 percent of their mental energy is going to decoding. This doesn't leave much for comprehending, responding, thinking, noticing, or enjoying. And it doesn't leave any for sounding fluent, which is something all those other things depend on. Demonstrate for children how you will naturally and appropriately sound disfluent as you do all the wonderful and necessary decoding work the first time you read a new book. Then read the same book again, attending to and thinking aloud about how your job this time is to make the words come out more smoothly now that you know what they are.

- *Readers reread when they want to think more about something in the book.* I can only listen to certain kinds of recorded books because most of the time I like to reread a passage here and there, and rewinding a book on my iPod is annoying. I was in a department store recently and saw a couple frantically running down the up escalator, having seen what they were looking for on the floor they were leaving and not wanting to go all the way up and around. I wonder if when newish readers pick up books they feel like they are on a one-way ride and cannot go back to reread. Or do they think their job is to merely finish their books, getting through as many as possible in the allotted time? You may need to tell children explicitly that books need not move in only one direction, like an airport walkway or an escalator. You probably already model this in read-alouds, but now is the time to be explicit, thinking aloud as you stop and reread: "Oh, that was confusing. I want to read that again." "Did you hear how lovely that sounded? I just need to read it again and really enjoy that language." "That was so funny! I'm going to read that again before moving on."

Are you getting the idea? This gives children the idea and the permission to spend their time savoring, as well as getting through, books.

● *Readers notice when the book gives them a strong feeling.* One of my hopes for my students is that they come to know and value the experience of being touched emotionally by a book. This goal comes through in read-aloud, where I can choose a variety of books and guide children through sophisticated concepts. Children can also achieve this in their independent reading, even if their books are simpler. I might say,

> I know we've been talking about the things that happen in our brains while we read. Today I want to talk about things that might happen in our hearts while we read. Yesterday I was talking to Susannah. She was reading *Biscuit*, by Alyssa Satin Capucilli, and found herself badly wanting a puppy of her own to play with and care for. Isn't it amazing that one of the books in her baggie could make such a strong feeling in Susannah's heart? I think it's so important for readers to notice when this happens that I decided to make a new bookmark. I'll put a few at each table so you can mark it to talk about later if your book gives you a strong feeling today.

● **Because** *is an important word to use when we share our thinking.* You may have already introduced this idea during read-aloud, but it can't hurt to remind children to be accountable for their thinking. Rather than setting aside a lesson for this concept, I try to draw attention to children who talk this way with their partners. I might stop the whole class for a moment to point out how much juicier a conversation has gotten because the children in that conversation are giving evidence for their thinking:

> Everyone, I want to tell you what I just heard over here. Amy and Kenji are talking about a book and it sounds like one of our read-aloud conversations! Amy said, "This dog doesn't even need an owner!" and Kenji asked her why she thought that, so Amy said, "*Because* he always has ideas to solve his problems on his own." She used that magic word, *because*. Wait, there's more. Then Kenji said, "But I think he still needs an owner *because* he needs someone to feed him. He never does that on his own." He used that magic word, too! Well, Amy and Kenji are still talking about

a really great question, so I'll let you all get back to work. As you do, see if the word *because* helps your conversations, too.

- **Thinking about the most important part can help us understand the book.** I've heard many teachers over the years encourage their students to share their favorite part or page with a partner. I must confess I'm a little on the fence about this time-honored activity. On the one hand, I know this can be an authentic reading behavior because I do it. On the other hand, when I listen to the conversations that center on this idea, they tend to go like this:

READER A: My favorite page is this one because it's funny. What's yours?

READER B: My favorite page is this one because I like the picture.

And then that's it. It seems to be a dead end, rather than an opening for more dialogue. As a way around this, I ask students to think and talk about the parts or pages they find most important in the book. This invites critical thought, as well as interesting conversation:

READER A: I think this page is most important because when the animals go back into the mud, they're doing what they always wanted to do.

READER B: I think this page is most important because Mrs. Wishy-Washy likes everything to be clean and this is where she gets the animals all clean.

Now this conversation might go somewhere. But even if it ends here, the thinking these children have done is crucial to developing an understanding of the meaning of the book and the qualities of the characters.

- **Partners can use their notes to help start a conversation.** Sometimes children know exactly what they want to discuss when partner time rolls around. Much of the time, they forget the powerful or captivating thoughts they had while reading. This is not a deficiency. I do the same thing if I'm not keeping track. We just need to teach children how to prepare for their partner conversations by looking back through their sticky notes or bookmarks and choosing one or two to spark a dialogue.

- **Partners can host a visit to one another's books.** This lesson comes straight from the brilliant mind of Kathy Collins, whom I thank abundantly for letting me write it here. Up to a certain point, children can share the same book in a partnership. By the time you get to this unit, many of your students will be past this point. If you don't have two copies of every single book in your library, you'll have to teach partners how to be true partners even if they have not yet read the same book. One way for children to talk authentically about a book only one of them has read is for that child to act as host. You might say,

> When your friend comes over for a play date, you are the host. To be a good host, you show them around your house: "Here's the bathroom for when you need it. Here's the kitchen if you get hungry for a snack." You introduce them to your family: "That's my sister. She's annoying. That's my dad. He's super fun, unless he's napping." And so on. The same goes for books. Tell your partner about the setting, the characters, the kind of story it is. But don't give away the juiciest parts!

Reflecting and Celebrating

I am always curious about how children are going to reflect on what they have learned in this unit. The work they have done is at once simple and in depth, age appropriate yet sophisticated. When they put their learning into their own words, it gives me a clear vision of what I can continue to expect and what needs to be reinforced over the next few units.

Guiding Questions

● *How are we more grown up as readers now than we were a month ago?* A question like this asks children to name the ways they have become stronger readers this month, and at the same time encourages them to take pride in this learning. It's a nice question to ask the whole class, because children often have a wide variety of answers. Among those I have heard are:

- I didn't used to listen to my brain while I was reading.
- I just used to think about what was happening, but not about the characters.
- I thought I was supposed to read without stopping.

All of these answers tell me that children are meeting my goals for them.

● *If a new student came into our class and asked, "What is reading?" what would you say?* This is a fascinating question. Children's answers to it can be a little funny, but I don't expect them to be able to articulate perfectly a process that many adults have trouble defining. Rather, I want exactly the six-year-old version that makes the most sense to them. At the end of this unit, I hope that the response includes ideas about thinking as well as decoding. Some of the answers I've heard are:

- Reading is, you look at the words and say them, and you think about them.
- Reading is when you see the story in your head.
- Reading can be words and pictures. You have to read words to read, but looking at the pictures also counts.
- Reading the words is only half of reading. The other half is thinking about the story.

■ Checking In

The next unit marks a big shift. This unit was primarily about process, and the next unit focuses on a genre. Many of the comprehension strategies in the next unit apply the thinking work of this unit specifically to nonfiction books. As children learn strategies specific to nonfiction reading, though, most of them will keep choosing some narratives or fictional stories in their baggies. In conferences and small groups, encourage children to keep doing the wonderful work they have begun to do in this unit in those books.

■ Professional Resources

Collins, Kathy. 2008. *Reading for Real: Teach Students to Read with Power, Intention, and Joy in K–3 Classrooms.* Portland, ME: Stenhouse.

STUDENTS' WORK SHOWS THAT I . . .	NEED TO TEACH OR RETEACH THIS TO THE WHOLE CLASS	NEED TO REMIND CHILDREN OF THIS SKILL	NEED TO TEACH THIS TO A SMALL GROUP OR IN A CONFERENCE	NEED TO CONGRATULATE CHILDREN FOR HOW WELL THEY DID IT
CHILDREN:				
Continue to dramatize books or parts of books	☐	☐	☐	☐
Maintain literal comprehension	☐	☐	☐	☐
Think while they read about any of the following things that are appropriate: • What is happening in the book • What they are learning • Their prior knowledge • Their questions • Their predictions • What the book reminds them of	☐	☐	☐	☐
Infer where necessary	☐	☐	☐	☐
Have and share opinions about their books	☐	☐	☐	☐
Begin to monitor their comprehension	☐	☐	☐	☐
Use decoding strategies with greater flexibility	☐	☐	☐	☐
Discuss their thoughts with partners	☐	☐	☐	☐
Prepare for partner talk by using tools to keep track of their thinking	☐	☐	☐	☐
Read their partners' books	☐	☐	☐	☐
Talk and think together about books both partners have read	☐	☐	☐	☐
Keep track of their thinking	☐	☐	☐	☐
Talk about books after reading them	☐	☐	☐	☐
Participate in class conversations about books	☐	☐	☐	☐
Share their learning processes and make helpful or encouraging questions or comments during share sessions	☐	☐	☐	☐

Figure 4–5 Student Work Chart

Supporting the Unit

Read Aloud with Purposeful Talk

Your students are probably getting better at sticking to one or two topics, adding to and extending one another's thoughts, and supporting their own ideas with evidence from the text. Rather than push for more skills, give children more time to work on the following qualities of good conversation.

- Children can ask questions to clarify what they hear ("What do you mean?" or "What makes you think that?").

- Children can agree or disagree, giving evidence from the text ("I don't think so because _____." Or "I thought the same thing because _____.").

- Children can suggest ideas they are not sure about, to see what the group thinks ("I'm not sure, but I think that maybe _____. Was anybody else thinking about that?").

It is also important to continue to support the work of thinking while reading in the context of read-aloud.

- Use sticky notes or bookmarks to record kinds of thinking, as you introduce these to the class.

- Think aloud in different ways in response to your reading.

- Invite children to stretch their repertoire, asking them to think in ways you may not have seen them do before.

Shared Reading: Practicing Print Strategies

In this unit, you may need to introduce and practice more advanced print strategies through shared reading. You can determine what these should be based on the reading levels of your students. You might find some of the following helpful:

- When one strategy doesn't work, try another.

- Recognize bigger chunks, such as roots or affixes.

- Use analogy more quickly (I know _____, so this word must be _____).

Shared Reading: Thinking Together

Use some of your shared reading time to give children opportunities to think about what they are reading as a group.

- Choose some big books that have strong characters or interesting plots. Invite children to help you record class ideas on large sticky notes or bookmarks.

- Guide children in putting their thoughts into words.

Working with Advanced Readers

The content of this unit is designed for all levels of students. You will find enough to keep your more advanced students challenged in the unit itself. If you have a few students comfortably reading chapter books, you could support them further by launching a book club with them. Kathy Collins' wonderful book, *Reading for Real: Teach Students to Read with Power, Intention, and Joy in K–3 Classrooms,* is a powerful resource to help with this.

Working with Readers Who Are Having a Hard Time

For some readers, thinking about anything other than decoding while reading may not come naturally. Those children who are just beginning to get the hang of decoding will be particularly vulnerable in this unit. Guiding children in talking about their books in a small group may ease their discomfort. This may look something like a book club that revolves around books at early levels. Encourage them to talk about characters, compare books, and notice parts that provoke an emotional response. Brand New Readers (an imprint of Candlewick Press) are especially helpful.

This unit addresses fluency to the extent that it can be addressed in a whole-class context, based on my estimate that most first graders will be reading between levels F and J at this point in the year. Of course, there will always be students reading earlier and later levels. Work with these concepts will be either exposure or review for these students. It is vital to fine-tune your teaching around fluency through both small-group work and individual conferences, in order to best meet everyone's needs.

In the next unit, you will ask children to identify qualities they love in books. To prepare for this, ask them to jot a quick note about each book they read. It should simply give the title and author of the book (and the level if you want), whether they liked the book, and what they did or didn't like about it. They can leave these notes in their book baggies or in a specially designated envelope.

■ Goals/Outcomes

This unit is focused on developing and maintaining fluency. The goals balance comprehension and print work, as children need to negotiate both to become truly fluent readers. Habits and community goals still play an important role this month.

Making Meaning

We hope children will

- maintain a strong connection to meaning in the face of more difficult decoding challenges
- use meaning to support fluency

Decoding

We hope children will

- monitor visually (check that what they are reading matches what they see on the page)
- use analogy to decode new words (notice familiar parts of unfamiliar words)
- use their growing repertoire of sight words to read both familiar and new words with greater automaticity

Habits

We hope children will

- attend to how they sound when they read, both aloud and silently

- continue to notice and reread rough spots in their reading

Community

We hope children will

- share an interest in and respect of one another's learning

- share with partners and with the class how they have been working on fluency

- offer and accept help from classmates

■ Getting Ready to Teach

In preparing for this unit, think ahead about what books or enlarged texts you'll need to support your teaching. Your most recent formal assessment data might be a little out of date, and your next opportunity to collect data might still be a few weeks off. Make sure you have a handle on your children's current reading levels, if you need to, by doing quick running records in unfamiliar texts. I have written many of the lessons based on an assumption that the majority of children in your class will be reading between levels F and J at this point in the year, with some reading before or after these levels.

Gathering Materials

No special materials are needed for this unit if your children are appropriately matched to books they enjoy. In preparation for the final unit, however, you might ask children to jot responses to their books on sticky notes or small slips of paper. Give each child an envelope, which can be kept in the book baggy, to keep these notes together. These need not be lengthy responses. A short note, such as "I like this book because it is funny", "I like tomboys," or "I want to find more books by this author" is all children will need going into the next unit.

Considering Students

The lessons in the first section of this study will be appropriate for children reading between levels F and J. If the majority of your students, or even a significant minority of them, reads levels earlier or later than this, you will want to rethink the print strategies you teach. Pinnell and Fountas' *Continuum of Literacy Learning* (2007) is an excellent resource for targeting reading strategies to readers at particular levels.

Preparing Demonstration Materials

Look through the teaching ideas, thinking about how to use the materials available to you to illustrate concepts. For the first section of the study, you will need to compile a list of words that your students will likely need help decoding, preferably taken right from their books. Try to find a book or passage for each lesson now, before you begin, so that you'll have time to get it into a format that's large enough for your class to see.

Choosing Books to Help You Teach

In the first part of the study, use books at your students' reading levels. Choose different types of books (fiction, nonfiction, rhyming, repetitive, humorous, serious, etc.) so that children practice using the variety of strategies you'll teach. You will need to find texts with good dialogue, strong characters, and clear moods for the second section of the study. Here is a list of some specific titles mentioned in this chapter, but you may discover many others that are just as effective.

- *Biscuit Wins a Prize* by Alyssa Satin Capucilli

- *Pedro's Burro* by Alyssa Satin Capucilli

- *Charlie Is Broken* based on the original Charlie and Lola stories by Lauren Child

- *More Spaghetti I Say* by Rita Golden Gelman and Mort Gerberg

- *Itchy, Itchy Chicken Pox* by Grace Maccarone and Betsy Lewin

- *Shortcut* by Donald Crews

- *Roller Coaster* by Marla Frazee

Teaching

Solving Problems as We Go

At this point in their reading development, children need to solve problems on the run, without having to slow down too much. Some difficult words will still bring their reading to a halt, but for the most part children should only have to slow down to figure out new words, and then they resume their regular pace. The following strategies are designed to help children maintain a good reading rate and read smoothly.

Topics for Lessons, Conferences, or Mid-Workshop Focus Points

● *Seeing bigger chunks can help readers figure out harder words.* As children's reading levels increase, the words they encounter in their books become more challenging. The print strategies you taught in the fall are no longer adequate for these new challenges. Teach children that they are now capable of looking at bigger groups of letters to help them figure out bigger words. You might first want to demonstrate this and have children practice it with some preselected words written on a chart in isolation. The next day, reinforce the strategy by looking at words in context, enlarging some pages from books in your library on a poster machine, document camera, overhead projector, or the old-fashioned way (writing it yourself on a chart). Look for longer words, ideally in books like those most of your children are reading. A quick scan of a few books I have on my shelf, which children might be reading toward the end of first grade, yielded the following words: *different, mountains, hospital, rosebud, mermaid, sometimes, decorate, wondering, enemy, excitement,* and *twitched.*

> Readers, I've been noticing that your books have longer words for you to figure out, but that many of you are still looking at chunks of just two or three letters. I want to show you how your eyes and brains are actually ready to see chunks of more letters. Watch what I do to figure out this word here. I could just look at the first two letters and say *so,* but if I look at a bigger chunk I see that this part of the word looks just like *come.* It must be *some.* Now I'm going to look at another bigger chunk. It's *time* with an *s. Times.* Putting at all together, I get *sometimes.* Just two chunks and an *s.* If I had tried to put together all these little chunks, I'd be saying "so me tim ease." That makes no sense at all! Here are a few more words for you to try right now while we're sitting here together. If you already know a word, skip it and try one you don't know. Tell me how you could break it into bigger chunks.

TIME FRAME	SECTION OF STUDY	WHAT CHILDREN DO	WHAT WE TEACH
6–8 days	Solving problems as we go	• Begin to use print strategies on the go, slowing down to solve words but not quite stopping • Learn print strategies required by the more challenging books they are now able to read • Focus on keeping their reading sounding smooth, even if they read silently	Topics for lessons, conferences, or mid-workshop focus points • Seeing bigger chunks can help readers figure out harder words. • As readers get stronger, they recognize a lot more chunks, or parts of words. • Readers try different vowel sounds when figuring out new words. • As they read harder books, readers let their eyes move ahead, taking in a few words at a time. • Sometimes readers skip a tricky word and come back to it. • When readers just can't figure out a word, they substitute a word that means something close so they can keep reading. • Readers smooth out rough patches by rereading. • Readers make sure that what they are reading matches what they see on the page. • Readers match their voices to the ending punctuation. • Readers pause at commas.
4–5 days	Matching sound to meaning	• Practice matching their expression and modulation to the content of their books	Topics for lessons, conferences, or mid-workshop focus points • Quotation marks tell readers when characters are talking. • Readers read dialogue with expression that matches the character's feelings. • Readers read dialogue to match what they know about the character's personality. • Readers pay attention to rhythm and rhyme. • Readers match their speed to the mood of what they are reading.
1 day	Reflecting and celebrating	• Read aloud a book, page, or passage they have worked to read with fluency	Guiding question • How are you now paying more attention to the sound of your reading?

Figure 6–1 Unit at a Glance

● *As readers get stronger, they recognize a lot more chunks, or parts of words.*
At this point in the year, most of your students probably recognize about 100 to 150 sight words. Point out to students that this means they can recognize not just whole words, but also a great many parts of words. If they know *around*, then they should also know, by sight, *-ound*. When children see the words *sound, astounded, surround*, and *bound*, they will have a head start on decoding the words if they know to isolate this chunk. Other frequently used words that help decode different words are *make, made, thing, could, right, write, long, most,*

place, *think*, *about*, *each*, and many more. Training students' eyes to see these familiar chunks in unfamiliar words takes time and practice. You can help by calling attention to it whenever you see words containing these chunks during shared reading.

● **Readers try different vowel sounds when figuring out new words.** Understanding vowels is one of the trickiest things about learning to read English. Each vowel makes several different sounds, they can all make the schwa sound, and the same vowel might sound different to people in different English-speaking areas. How do you pronounce the *o* in *on*? The *e* in *egg*? The *a* in *chance*?

Effective word solvers know that vowels work in mysterious ways, and they use this knowledge to their advantage. Teach children to try different vowel sounds when they are decoding new words. Usually just trying the short and long sounds will work. Even if children just get "in the ballpark," it will be close enough to the right word that they will be able to figure it out. Demonstrate how you pronounce the sounds of the letters, first one way and then another:

> Here's a word I'm going to have to think about. It looks like *win ding*. *Win ding* doesn't sound right, though. Let me try the long *i* sound. *Wine ding*. *Winding*. Yes, that sounds right and it makes sense here! Did you see how when the word I was saying didn't sound right to me I tried another sound for the vowel? I'm going to give you a chance to try it now. Here are some other words you may not know. When you read them, try different sounds for the vowel. Make sure to try the short and long sounds! I'll give you a minute to try it and then we'll talk about what you found out.

A look through a few first grade books I have on my shelf yielded some ideal words for demonstrating and practicing this strategy: *winding*, *cradle*, *skating*, *post*, and *tiny*.

● **As they read harder books, readers let their eyes move ahead, taking in a few words at a time.** For some children, this will come naturally, but for many others it needs to be taught. It's hard to demonstrate how your eyes scan and where they focus as you read. As readers of English, we focus on a horizontal band of the page that spans a few words. If I could stop time right as you are reading these words, we could highlight to illustrate exactly what your eyes are seeing. First graders aren't reading texts like this one, though. Luckily, most of their books are already organized to support them by having only a few words on each line. We don't have to teach them to focus on something as abstract as a band of words, but we do need to teach them to look at more than one word at a time.

Enlarge a page from a book or transcribe a page onto a chart pad, making sure to keep the line breaks as they are printed in the book. Demonstrate for children how you see all the words almost at the same time:

> I'm going to show you what's happening in my eyes and brain as I read this page. When I'm reading to myself, this happens very fast, but I'm going to let you see it in slow motion. Instead of seeing or reading one word at a time, I read a whole line at a time. Here on this line I see three words. My eyes see this whole line. Then when I *read* the line, all the words come out together. "My new school." That's why I sound so nice and smooth when I read. I'll do it again on the next line. First I see all the words, then I say all the words. "Has a big playground." Now you try it. See the whole next line and then say it aloud. Doesn't that sound so nice and smooth? Try this today in your own books.

● **Sometimes readers skip a tricky word and come back to it.** It doesn't pay to get hung up on a tricky word for too long. The story slips further and further away as we spend more time trying to figure out what the word is. Teach children that if a word is delaying them for more than a couple of seconds, the best tactic is to keep on reading. They can use the whole sentence, before *and* after the word in question, to make an educated guess of the word. It helps even to read the sentence at a good pace, saying "blank" in place of the tricky word. I might say, "Oh, this word is a new one for me! I know it starts like *gor*, but I can't get the rest of it. OK, I'm going to read the whole sentence and say 'blank' when I get to this word. 'She thought her blank new coat looked very nice.' Gor, hmm, *gorgeous*! That makes sense and sounds right. Now let me reread it. 'She thought her gorgeous new coat looked very nice.' Yes."

● **When readers just can't figure out a word, they substitute a word that means something close so they can keep reading.** I was recently talking to my friend Susan Choi, a writer of some note, having been a finalist to receive a Pulitzer Prize. She was talking about moving, and said that she was looking for a new place "in a desultory way." It can be hard talking to writers sometimes! I wasn't about to say, "Hang on, Susan, let me go get a dictionary." Luckily, it was part of a larger conversation, so I was able to infer that she meant something like "in a casual way," or "not that seriously," and move on. There are going to be words children just don't know, no matter how assiduously they apply the strategies we teach. I still encounter words I don't know from time to time, and have come across *desultory* many times without stopping to look it up. I teach children to do what works for me in this situation: think about what the unfamiliar word probably means, and move on. Teach them to put a sticky note exactly where the word was spotted so that it can be found in a dictionary at a later time, when it won't interrupt the flow of the story.

And, by the way, *desultory* means inconsistent, unplanned, random, or haphazard. My substitution wasn't exactly right, but it was close enough for me to maintain comprehension without interrupting the conversation.

● ***Readers smooth out rough patches by rereading.*** Although we have been teaching children to solve problems on the run, sometimes children have to stop, think, and maybe even backtrack. This is reflected in the previous two strategies. Teach children that, just as they learned early in the year when they were reading very different books, they should still be rereading after solving a problem. Hearing the flow of the text is important to keeping a strong connection to comprehension.

● ***Readers make sure that what they are reading matches what they see on the page.*** You have taught children to monitor visually in the past, but it bears mentioning again as part of a discussion of fluency. Visual monitoring looks different in the reader of level H texts than it does in the reader of level C texts. When you taught visual monitoring earlier in the year, you were more concerned that children noticed if a word they thought might be *rabbit* was actually *bunny*. You needed children to look at the word as opposed to just the picture. Children reading level H are scanning the text more actively with their eyes, able quickly to notice subtler differences in what they are reading and what they are seeing. Now you need them to notice differences like the one between *rabbit* and *rabbits*. You also need them to notice these differences in a way that doesn't bring their reading to a halt, but maybe just puts a little hiccup into it.

I want to show you how sometimes readers notice that the page says something a little different than what they just read, so they can quickly fix it. You know how when I'm reading aloud to you, sometimes I make a little mistake and quickly correct it? That happens to readers all the time. Even grown-ups who have been reading for many years sometimes make a little mistake. What happens to me is that I say something, then my eyes see that the page says something a little different, and then I say the right thing. It just happened earlier when I was reading this Biscuit book, so I marked the page to show you. I said, "Biscuit waits—wants to see the fish." You see, *waits* and *wants* look a lot alike, so I just thought I saw *waits*. Then my eyes quickly told me it was *wants*. So I just corrected it right then and there. This was not really a rough patch so I don't need to go back and reread the whole thing. If *you* are reading and *your* eyes tell you the page says something different, like my eyes told me, you might be able to fix it quickly and keep reading.

That was from *Biscuit Wins a Prize* by Alyssa Satin Capucilli, by the way.

● ***Readers match their voices to the ending punctuation.*** Up to a point in children's books, sentences end at the end of a line of print. As children's books get more difficult, they might see a wider variety of punctuation, placed more unpredictably on the page. This means that some children stop reading at the end of a line, even if the sentence is not finished, or that they read right through periods placed in the middle of a line. Teach children to pay close attention to how sentences end, noticing that this may happen right in the middle of a line. Show them how to stop briefly at periods, add some excitement for exclamation points, and inflect appropriately for questions.

A question mark doesn't always mean "Make your voice go up," so knowing how to inflect depends on meaning. Consider these two questions:

● How is he doing?

● Is she here yet?

In the first my voice goes down, whereas in the second my voice rises. The most important information given by a question mark is that a sentence has ended, and that it was asking a question. If children are paying attention to the meaning of the text, their inflection will likely be appropriate.

● ***Readers pause at commas.*** Commas start appearing in pretty early levels, though we may not need to teach explicitly how to read them until later in the year. Even now it may make more sense to address commas in shared reading. If a lot of your students are starting to notice commas (or other punctuation) in their books, gather them for a lesson on how commas affect the sound of our reading. I do not think it necessary or appropriate to discuss things like compound sentences or independent clauses, but it is perfectly reasonable to teach children to pause ever so briefly at a comma.

Matching Sound to Meaning

This section of the study shifts from problem solving to expression. Children should learn to make their voices express the mood or rhythm of a text and the personality of a character. Explain to children that this comes directly out

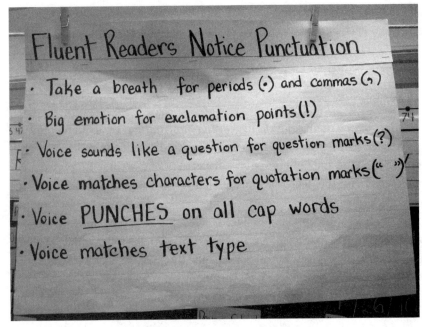

Figure 6–2 Fluent Readers Notice Punctuation

of the work they did with dramatization in the "Bringing Books to Life" unit. They should apply that same sense of fun and creativity to reading texts with fluency. You may ask children to focus on how they sound as they read aloud, but it is also important to teach them to attend to how they sound when they read silently. How we sound when we read aloud is pretty much how our internal voice sounds when we read silently.

Topics for Lessons, Conferences, or Mid-Workshop Focus Points

● *Quotation marks tell readers when characters are talking.* The lessons that follow require children to be aware of dialogue in their books. You may need to teach, at least to a small group, how to identify dialogue in a text. Read a big book or other enlarged text that contains some dialogue. As you read, think aloud about how the quotation marks cue you to read certain parts as the character might say them:

> I was just reading this book with Aaron earlier, and we noticed that the author was actually letting us hear the characters talking, so we had to read it with their voices. Let's look at the part Aaron was noticing. It says, "Lola is trying to do somersaults. She says . . ." and here is where we see the quotation marks. This tells us that the next words are Lola's

Figure 6–3 Remind students that writers sometimes give clues describing how characters sound.

words and that when we read these words, we should sound a little like Lola. "She says, 'It's not working, Charlie. You have to push me.'" Did you hear how I read it? The quotation marks told me to do that. When you notice quotation marks, make sure to read the words inside them as if you are the character.

● *Readers read dialogue with expression that matches the character's feelings.* One concrete way into developing expression is to work on dialogue. Using an enlarged text, show children how you use what you know about characters' feelings or intentions to inform how your voice sounds when you read their words:

A lot of the books in our classroom library are stories with dialogue. That means that when we read them, we can practically hear the characters talking. I want to show you how my reading makes most sense and sounds best when I match how I read dialogue to how I know a character is feeling. Remember this book, *Pedro's Burro* (by Alyssa Satin Capucilli)? On this page, I remember that Pedro is a little worried that he and his father won't be able to find a burro. He says, "How will we ever find a burro that is just right?" If I say it just like that though, it doesn't sound very worried. Now, when I read it again, I am going to read it with a worried or anxious voice. Listen to how it sounds this time. "How will we ever find a burro that is just right?" Do you hear the difference? You can do that too. When you read dialogue, think about how the character is feeling, and see if you can make your voice show that feeling.

- **Readers read dialogue to match what they know about the character's personality.** Taking the previous lesson to another level, show children how you read with expression that matches not just the feelings of a character but also the personality. Knowing if a character is nice or mean, playful or tired, silly or serious should figure into how children read his dialogue. Again, using an enlarged text, demonstrate for children how you think about a character's traits and then match your voice to what you know:

> Remember how we were saying that Lola is a tiny bit bossy, or at least that she definitely knows what she wants? I'm going to think about that when I read this bit of her dialogue here. "It's not working, Charlie. You have to push me." I am trying to make it sound like Lola's really the one talking! If I thought Lola were a whiny girl, I might make it sound like this: [deliver line in whiny fashion], or if I thought she were shy, I might make it sound like this: [deliver line in shy fashion]. Those don't sound like the Lola I know. Can you see how knowing what a character is like helps us read her dialogue really well?

- **Readers pay attention to rhythm and rhyme.** Many books in a first grade library use rhythm or rhyme, or both, as a support for young readers. Unfortunately, children who are still starting out as readers may not notice the cadence. Teach children that if they notice a couple of rhyming words in what they read, it may be a clue that it is a rhyming book, and should be read in a certain way. They may have to go back and reread a few lines to confirm whether this is true. You will have to demonstrate this so children know exactly what you mean. "Sometimes books have rhyming words, and they sound a little like a chant when we read them. Many of these books don't tell you they have rhymes before you start reading them, and it's easy not to notice it. I'm going to show you how, when I notice that a book has rhymes in it, I go back and see if I also need to read it with a rhythm." Read a page or two of something like *More Spaghetti I Say*, by Rita Golden Gelman and Mort Gerberg or *Itchy, Itchy Chicken Pox*, by Grace Maccarone and Betsy Lewin. Make sure to completely ignore the obvious rhythmic structure in your first read, so your second reading offers a big contrast. "'Black cat. Gray cat. Rich cat. Stray cat.' Did you hear that? *Stray* rhymes with *gray*. Let me go back and see if that is a clue that this book has a rhythm." Now read it as it was meant to be. "Wow! That's so much better! And as I keep reading, that rhythm and rhyme will help me. Not all books that have rhyming words will turn out to be books with a rhythm, but it's a good idea to check. I know we have a lot of them in this classroom, so if you come across one, let us all know!"

● *Readers match their speed to the mood of what they are reading.* There has been such an emphasis put on reading rate lately, and it is important for children to maintain a good rate. I don't want to inadvertently create a bunch of speed-readers though! Children shouldn't get so hung up on rate that they forget to think about what they are reading—what it means and how it feels. It makes sense to introduce this idea first in shared reading and later as a lesson for independent reading.

You demonstration might sound like this:

> OK, let me show you how I might slow down or speed up as I read, depending on the mood of the book. It almost feels like the book is *telling me* how to read it! Here, let's look at *Shortcut* by Donald Crews. We all know what happens very well. It's scary, and they all make a decision that they later wish they had made differently. Now look here at the end, after their big scare. "We didn't talk about what had happened for a long time. And we never took the shortcut again." Whenever I read that part, I read it slowly. It feels kind of sad, and like that feeling you get when you know you did something wrong. Maybe ashamed? Anyway, the feeling, or mood, tells me to slow down.
>
> Now, let's take a look at *Roller Coaster* by Marla Frazee. It seems to be moving along at a regular speed, or pace, until it slows down on this page and then takes off right here when the roller coaster goes down the big hill. Listen. "And then . . ." that part's still slow. "Whoosh! Most people scream. Some people can't make a sound. And one person can't even open her eyes." I have to read this part more quickly to keep up with the roller coaster! Do you see what I mean? Sometimes the mood of a book tells you to speed up or slow down your reading.

Reflecting and Celebrating

To celebrate this unit, invite children to read passages that they have worked on reading with greater fluency. This can be done in one or two workshop sessions depending on your class size and the length of the passages that children read. Ask each child to talk briefly about how the passage he chose reflects the work he is most proud of for the unit. The other children should pay special attention to this as they listen to their classmate's reading.

Guiding Question

● *How are you now paying more attention to the sound of your reading?* Children's answers to this question will tell you how they are internalizing and making sense of the importance of sound to the act of reading. Whether they read aloud or silently, their reading must still be fluent in order to support comprehension.

■ Checking In

In the next unit, you will be helping your class prepare for a summer of reading truly independently. If you asked them to keep notes on what they like about their favorite books, make sure children save the notes in a safe place. The students will refer to their notes as part of their summer planning. If you complete a more formal assessment this month, such as the Developmental Reading Assessment or Fountas and Pinnell Benchmark Assessment System, these data will also support children's ability to choose books well during the summer.

■ Professional Resources

Pinnell, Gay Su, and Irene C. Fountas. 2007. *The Continuum of Literacy Learning, Grades K–2: A Guide to Teaching.* Portsmouth, NH: Heinemann.

Rasinski, Timothy V. 2003. *The Fluent Reader: Oral Reading Strategies for Building Word Recognition, Fluency, and Comprehension.* New York: Scholastic.

STUDENTS' WORK SHOWS THAT I . . .	NEED TO TEACH OR RETEACH THIS TO THE WHOLE CLASS	NEED TO REMIND CHILDREN OF THIS SKILL	NEED TO TEACH THIS TO A SMALL GROUP OR IN A CONFERENCE	NEED TO CONGRATULATE CHILDREN FOR HOW WELL THEY DID IT
CHILDREN:				
Maintain a strong connection to meaning in the face of more difficult decoding challenges	☐	☐	☐	☐
Use meaning to support fluency	☐	☐	☐	☐
Monitor visually (check that what they are reading matches what they see on the page)	☐	☐	☐	☐ ☐
Use analogy to decode new words (notice familiar parts of unfamiliar words)	☐	☐	☐	☐
Use their growing repertoire of sight words to read both familiar and new words with greater automaticity	☐	☐	☐	☐
Attend to how they sound when they read, both aloud and silently	☐	☐	☐	☐
Continue to notice and reread rough spots in their reading	☐	☐	☐	☐
Share an interest in and respect of one another's learning	☐	☐	☐	☐
Share with partners and with the class how they have been working on fluency	☐	☐	☐	☐

Figure 6–4 Student Work Chart

Supporting the Unit

Read Aloud with Purposeful Talk

Continue to develop strong conversational skills, reading aloud both fiction and nonfiction texts. Children's conversational skills may be so strong at this point that you are better served to sit aside and listen, intervening only when necessary to keep the peace, get back on track, insert an idea of your own, or remind everyone that it's time for recess. In taking a less active role, guide children toward sharing their ideas, if possible, without needing to raise their hands.

- Listen to the conversation the class is having. If you have an idea to share, say it when you hear a pause. If you don't have an idea to share, it's OK to keep listening.

- If you are holding onto an idea and the conversation moves in a different direction, you might have to table your thought for a future conversation.

This is a good time to bring the dramatization work back to fiction texts.

- Stop at particularly strong scenes between characters to ask children to repeat the dialogue with expression.

- In particularly emotional sections of text, model matching your rate and expression to the mood.

Shared Reading: Sounding Like Readers Together

Rather than using a lot of big books in this unit, enlarge a variety of pages of books you have read aloud and with which your class is familiar. Choose pages that have either rich dialogue or a clear mood or tone. Practice reading these together with appropriate vocalization, considering both rate and expression.

Partnership: Being Directors and Actors

Partners in this unit can work together to read pages, passages, stories, or poems with appropriate fluency and expression. Where necessary, partners should continue to help one another use effective print strategies.

- Partners can remind one another to connect to the feeling of a character's dialogue.

- Partners can tell one another if they're going overboard.

- Partners can act out scenes between two characters, reading the dialogue together.

Working with More Advanced Readers

Starting at around level I, it's appropriate to expect readers to begin reading silently. Some children will pick this up immediately. Others may need to whisper their reading for a while, and then move their lips silently for a while. It's important to meet with these children as a group to explain a few things about silent reading. You might say:

- When we read "inside our heads," we still need to pay just as much attention to fluency as people who read aloud.

- It is even more important to monitor silent reading because no one else will hear or be able to fix an error.

- Reading silently doesn't always mean reading fast. We still have to match our rate to the mood of the text.

- If you do have to stop to decode a word, it can help to try it out loud. It's still important to reread the whole sentence in this case.

- You might need to slow down for unfamiliar words, but try not to stop. Let your eyes continue to take in more than one word at a time.

- Sometimes the part of a book that is *not* dialogue suggests a strong feeling. Try to match your expression to this mood, just like you do with the parts that *are* dialog.

Working with Readers Who Are Having a Hard Time

Children who are reading a few levels below what you think of as grade level at this point in the year are still going to need support in using decoding strategies. They may also need additional support reading with fluency. Pull small groups as necessary to work on the following:

- If you have multiple copies of an appropriate title, it can help for children to listen to one another read the same passage.

- Children can work in partnerships to read and perform dialogue with expression.

- If you have the means to record children reading, they can listen critically to their own voices.

7

Planning for Independence and Summer Reading

I read all year, but there's something different about summer reading. Maybe it's being able to read for hours at a time without the guilt of knowing I should be doing something else. Maybe it's the way books are marketed differently during the summer. Maybe it's just the weather. It feels easier somehow to get all wrapped up in the world of a book. Summer reading is more, well, *natural*. Late in the spring, I start compiling my stack. I ask for recommendations, look at book reviews a little more carefully, and see what my local bookstore has on the "staff favorites" shelf. I might make a late addition if something comes to my attention during the summer. It just gets added to the stack. Sometimes I'm too ambitious and my stack takes me into the fall. That's all OK. Planning the stack wouldn't be so much fun for me if I couldn't be flexible about how I read it.

As a teacher, I feel lucky to be the first to introduce children to what will hopefully become a rite of summer for them as it is for me: Planning the Stack. In this unit, I have tried to make my own stack-planning process appropriate for first graders. You may have your own way of planning for summer reading, and I encourage you to inject as much of your own personality and preferences as will fit into the unit. If your students see you as a passionate reader, whose most delicious reading time is when school is out, they may more easily cast themselves in that role as well.

■ Overview

As a classroom teacher, I often had an uphill climb trying to actually teach anything in June. It was hot, we had trips and picnics planned, final assessments and report cards had to be done, and all of us knew we were on the threshold of the most magical of times—summer vacation. The best way I found to use this time was to help children move toward reading without the support of a strong learning community. This unit is designed to last for the last three to four weeks of school, with the recognition that this month often makes it difficult to teach. There are fewer teaching ideas than days to teach, which means you and your class can talk about some of the concepts over a few days. The goal is not so much for children to learn new strategies or increase reading levels, but rather to prepare for independence. Do this by asking children to recognize their reading identities and to get familiar with the resources available to them for getting reading material. The unit begins with a look back on how far they have come as readers and ends with a celebration of who they have yet to become as they continue to grow.

■ Goals/Outcomes

The main goals of this unit focus on developing strong reading habits, though of course we want our students leaving us as well-rounded readers.

Making Meaning

We hope children will

- name qualities they look for when choosing books

- continue to engage with their books as they've learned to do all year

Decoding

We hope children will

- continue to work on the strategies required by their books

Habits

We hope children will

- choose books with purpose, based on qualities they enjoy

- plan and choose books for future reading

- learn about nearby resources for getting reading material

- identify friends or peers who share reading tastes

Community

We hope children will

- share ideas about different qualities of book

- make and share book recommendations

- identify and appreciate ways that individual members of the community have grown this year

■ Getting Ready to Teach

Like the other units, this one requires a little preparation. Gather or create any materials you'll need for this unit, and make sure children have access to appropriate books for the whole time. Many teachers start packing up their rooms before the year is over. Feel free to put away all those books that were so indispensable in September, but please hold off on the ones that are just now getting their day in the sun!

Gathering Materials

Your students will continue to need access to appropriate books. Besides this, they will need the envelope of notes they collected about their books in the previous unit. I have suggested some sheets children can fill out as part of this unit, to help them and their parents or caregivers during the summer. If you decide to use these, or would prefer to make your own, make the copies ahead of time so that you can hand them out early in the unit. Though not necessary, it's nice to send children home on the last day of school with their own book baggies, to make explicit the connection between home and school reading. Gallon freezer bags work well. It's also nice to create and decorate a special folder for the sheets they'll be filling out, so don't put away your art supplies too early!

Considering Students

You probably have just completed or are about to complete your final round of formal assessments for the year. Use this information not just to help your children continue to choose just-right books in school, but to help them plan their summer reading. The world outside of school does not organize itself according to book levels, and we want children to be able to choose books for themselves in a library or bookstore, which will not have conveniently marked baskets of levels of books. Use your most recent assessment data to teach children instead to look inside of books and recognize the many ways a book can be just right.

Preparing Demonstration Materials

In this unit, you will not demonstrate a lot of new strategies. You will show children how to find books independently that are just right for them and how to get their hands on reading materials. Look through the lesson topics before you start the unit. These will guide you in researching the resources most appropriate for your class. Look up your local library's address and phone number. If you can, invite the children's librarian to visit your class and explain how to get library cards and any other resources for summer reading the library might offer. Check out the websites I suggest in Appendix B, and look for any that are more specific to your locality, such as those sponsored by state government, a local library system, or your school system. Write down the names and addresses of all the bookstores in your area, new or used, that specialize in children's books. Doing all of this ahead of time will make the unit go more smoothly.

Choosing Books to Help You Teach

Consider bringing your own stack of books you plan to read during the summer, so you can talk to your class about how you chose each one. If you can, bring books you chose for a variety of reasons—favorite author, topic of interest, genre you love, and so on.

This is a good month to read aloud a few stories about characters who love to read. David McPhail's *Edward in the Jungle* and *Edward and the Pirates* feature a voracious reader who literally gets immersed in the world of a book. Colin Thompson's *How to Live Forever* takes place in a magical world of books that comes to life in the library after closing time. This has some neat references for adult readers, too. *The Old Woman Who Loved to Read* by John Winch is about a woman who, yes, loves to read, so much so that no matter what life throws her way, she tackles it with a book in hand. Books such as these will help you get conversations going not just about reading, but about *being a reader*—in or out of school.

■ Teaching

We Are All Readers

This phrase calls to mind the first section of the first unit. Bring the year full circle by letting children know that they will always be readers. This section of the unit is as much about reflecting back on how far they have come as it is about thinking ahead about how they will express their identities as readers during the long summer vacation. They will belong to a very different reading community than that of the class, if they have one outside of school at all. Instead of feeling adrift and alone (and maybe giving up reading altogether for the summer), with your help children can see this as a time simply to enjoy reading. It may be a novel idea (pun not intended) to read purely for pleasure, without concern as to level, but this is exactly what summer reading is all about! Take the time now to help children discover and define their reading identities by thinking about how they can choose books independently.

Guiding Question

● *Who have we become as readers?* Allow children a while to think and talk about this. Ask them to consider who they used to be as readers way back in September, as a way to appreciate the distance they have come. Give them a sheet of paper with room for pictures and words, which they can keep by their side for a few days (there's a sample in Appendix A–3). They might even take the paper home to discuss with a parent or other caregiver. As children come up with ideas, they can pull out the paper and add to it. At the end of a few days, come together as a class and share children's ideas. It's important to give time and energy to this, because children's self-defined identities as readers are going to be the difference between reading and not reading during the vacation.

TIME FRAME	SECTION OF STUDY	WHAT CHILDREN DO	WHAT WE TEACH
4–5 days	We are all readers	• Think about and describe who they have become as readers • Identify some favorite books and some books that support growth • Plan a list of books, or kinds of books, to read on their own over the summer	Guiding question • Who have we become as readers? Topics for lessons, conferences, or mid-workshop focus points • Knowing what we love about our favorite books can help us plan for future reading. • Knowing what makes a book just right can help us plan for future reading. • Readers sometimes plan a whole stack of books to read. • Readers can plan books they want to listen to someone else read.

5–7 days	Planning for independence	• Learn about resources for getting books and think about how best to read on their own
		• Write a note to the next year's teacher describing their reading lives
			Topics for lessons, conferences, or mid-workshop focus points
			• Readers know how to get their hands on books.
			  • friends or family members who read similar books
			  • libraries
			  • bookstores, for both new and used books
			  • Internet
			• Readers know how to find things to read that are not books.
			• Letting next year's teacher know about you as a reader will make it easier for him or her to get you what you need.

3 days	Reflecting, celebrating, and saying good-bye	• Look back on their year together, thinking about how the community and individual students have grown as readers	Guiding question • How will you keep growing as a reader?

Figure 7–1 Unit at a Glance

Topics for Lessons, Conferences, or Mid-Workshop Focus Points

● *Knowing what we love about our favorite books can help us plan for future reading.* Besides friends, I depend on blurbs and reviews to help me choose books (OK, I admit I will sometimes pick a book because I like the cover art). There are qualities I look for in a book (well-crafted writing comes to mind), and other qualities I utterly avoid (not a big fan of the bodice ripper, the scary monster, or the conspiracy theory). I also go through phases—funny books, epic novels, true narrative accounts of disasters, particular authors, and so on. These phases usually start with a single book that grabs me and guides me through a few others. After a friend recommended *Corelli's Mandolin* (long before the movie came out, so I had never heard of it), I found myself reading four other books by Louis de Bernieres all in a row. So it seems natural to teach children that readers out there in the world make plans for their reading, based on what they love to read. If you have been asking children for a few weeks to jot a quick note about each book they finish (as suggested on page 119 of the previous unit), students can use these notes to help them fill out the sheet mentioned in the previous lesson. This list will be fodder for great classroom dialogue about books, will help children choose books for the last couple of weeks of school, and will later help the adults in their lives assist children to find books.

● ***Knowing what makes a book just right can help us plan for future reading.*** Children tend to think of *just right* as a phrase that describes a book's level. There's so much more to being just right than level, though. Certainly level is one criterion for "rightness." A book also has to be interesting to the reader. It may help to chart the considerations readers might take into account in choosing books. Author, character, series, genre, theme—these are all aspects of books that can either draw us in or keep us at arm's length. As you add items to the chart, invite children to share their tastes with one another. This is a great time to teach children about book reviews and recommendations. Students can give quick oral reviews of books (for instance, the *Little Bill* series by Bill Cosby and Varnette P. Honeywood and the *Pinky and Rex* books by James Howe and Melissa Sweet), letting their classmates know that "If you like *Little Bill*, you'll probably like *Pinky and Rex*, too. They also deal with realistic problems in a way that sometimes makes me laugh."

Appendix A–4 has a sheet each child can fill out with information about what is just right for him or her. A librarian or bookstore clerk can help children find books with these qualities. The chart will also help children focus if they flip though a few pages of a book to see if it's a good choice.

● ***Readers sometimes plan a whole stack of books to read.*** You have been asking children to do this all year. Every time children exchange what's in their baggies for a new set of books, they're planning a stack to read over a week's time. This lesson does not introduce a new idea as much as it draws a connection between school life and home life. Tell children that the two previous lessons have prepared them to have home baggies, which they will fill and refill all by themselves. You may show children your own stack of summer books, if you have had time to dream it up yet, and talk through how you made the choices you did. Give students some time to think about what they would love to have in their own summer baggies, if they could have whatever they wanted.

- **Readers can plan books they want to listen to someone else read.** It should be clear both to parents and to children that listening to books read aloud is also valuable summer reading time. It could be a book read by an actor on the Internet, a book on CD or DVD borrowed from the library, or an old-fashioned bedtime read-aloud by a parent, babysitter, or older sibling. Listening to books gives children access to more complicated stories than they might be able to read independently, it allows them to enjoy books without doing any of the work required for decoding or fluency, and it creates opportunities for discussion. Invite children to think about some of the books they would love to hear read aloud over the summer, and include these in children's summer plans so parents and caregivers can participate.

Planning for Independence

You've helped children make plans for what they want to read. Now it's time to help them figure out how to get reading materials. In this part of the study, you'll prepare children to be as proactive as possible for a six-year-old. Teach them about all the places in your area where children may find books, and guide them in enlisting an adult to help them get what they need.

Topics for Lessons, Conferences, or Mid-Workshop Focus Points

- **Readers know how to get their hands on books.** Over the next few days, teach children about the resources available in your area for getting reading material. There isn't much children can do in the classroom to practice using this information, so they'll probably read and enjoy their books on these days. It's helpful to have an ongoing conversation, though, because the idea of *needing to get one's hands on books* should be part of everyone's consciousness on the last day of school. You may want to help children record some of this information on a resource sheet (Appendix A–5 has a sample), which they can give to a parent or caregiver. I know it feels like a lot of sheets, but I've found it helpful to make double-sided copies with "What Is Just Right for Me?" on one side and "Reading Resources" on the other.
  - **Friends or family members who read similar books.** People in my section of Brooklyn have a habit of leaving bags or boxes of books out on the sidewalk when they're done reading them, so others can read them. Sometimes I find great books, and sometimes I'm disappointed I bent over to look. One of my neighbors, without fail, leaves books I want to read.

I now walk my dog past that house every night just so I can be the first responder when a new batch of books comes out. I also want students to know which of *their* friends (or siblings or cousins) read books that they might like, so they can try to arrange play/book swap dates with these children during the summer. Enlist the help of parents, if you can, to get names and phone numbers so children can make these connections.

- *Libraries.* One of my favorite community resources for books is the good old-fashioned library. While many libraries suffer from a lack of financial support, they still try to provide as much support to their local readers as they can. This means having as good a selection of books as possible, librarians who can help children find and choose books, volunteers who can tutor young readers, story times for different ages, and a variety of children's magazines. If your area has a local library with a good children's section, write down the address and phone number on the original form before you copy it for children.

- *Bookstores, for both new and used books.* Trading and borrowing books is a cheap, fun, and effective way to get one's hands on reading material. There is something to be said of acquiring a new, shiny, clean, undog-eared, and did I say new, book—to be the first one to run your fingers lightly across the still-smooth paper or gaze lovingly on the still-vibrant illustrations. If there happens to be a few extra dollars in the family coffer, I want children to know exactly where to go to find books they'll love.

When I was little I wasn't so keen on the hand-me-down clothes of my four older siblings. Their old books were another matter entirely. New books are certainly special, but somehow a preowned book is also special. I must have inherited this attitude toward used books from my parents, and I'm thankful for it. They definitely modeled reading, rereading, borrowing, trading, and buying used books. I've tried to pass along this appreciation to children by expressing the same copious gratitude for each book we've received as a gift, new or preloved.

If you can do the research, it will make it that much easier for parents to support their children over the summer. A list of resources might mean the difference between a child getting reading material over the summer and doing without. My neighborhood has one major chain bookstore and one locally owned bookstore, both with good children's sections. We also have several used bookstores, but only one of these specializes in children's books. With just a little bit of legwork, I can get the addresses and phone numbers of these stores onto the sheet of resources. Doesn't that sound easy and worthwhile?

- *Internet.* In some areas, it may be hard to get to a bookstore or library. Websites that sell books often have discounted prices or coupons that parents can use. I do believe that children can read all summer without spending a dime, but for those who can afford it, buying books on the Internet can be fun. Or at least, receiving an anxiously awaited package and ripping it open to find a great book can be fun.

● ***Readers know how to find things to read that are not books.*** I'm sure we all remember that tattered copy of *Highlights* from the dentist's office. Who could forget Goofus and Gallant? Most libraries have a good selection of magazines for children, on a variety of topics at a range of levels. My local library has a comfortable area for children to read, with miniature sofas and beanbag chairs. Magazines usually can't be checked out, but if a child happens to fall in love with *Ranger Rick* or *Spider*, a parent might be persuaded to fill out the subscription card.

Websites also provide great opportunities to read. Many children find motivation to read because they want to navigate websites without having to ask for help every three minutes. A few good websites, for those with Internet access, can keep children actively reading for a while. Some sites give access to hundreds of printable books for a fee, some feature actors reading books aloud, some provide book recommendations based on individual input, such as grade level and interests. I have included a few of the many resources available in Appendix B.

● ***Letting next year's teacher know about you as a reader will make it easier for him or her to get you what you need.*** Even with everything you have done to facilitate continued reading over the summer, it is still summer. Children will, as they should, spend most of their time running, playing, swimming, yelling, visiting, and generally getting in touch with their wild sides. They may forget what gave them so much pleasure as readers at the end of this year. They may show up to a new school year a little nervous about how it's going to go. If their teacher can provide even one familiar favorite, as you tried to do at the beginning of this year, it will help ease their minds. Invite your children to jot just a few sentences to next year's teacher, even if you don't know who that person is, listing favorite books, genres, or themes.

Reflecting, Celebrating, and Saying Good-bye

Here we are at the final, bittersweet section of the final unit of the year! I hope you take the time to celebrate your own accomplishments alongside those of your children. Take some time to tell children the many specific way you are proud of them, and invite them to share with one another the ways they plan to keep growing as readers.

Guiding Question

● *How will you keep growing as a reader?* You have helped children create lists of resources for themselves to facilitate summer reading. The ball is now in their court. By asking this question, you not only state your firm belief that everyone *will* grow as a reader, but you also open up a powerful conversation. When children exchange ideas about their plans for summer reading, they begin to take ownership of their reading lives. Some of the responses I have heard are:

- I'm going to bring books to every play date, to see if I can swap with my friend.
- I'm going to bring my books to the used bookstore to see if I can swap for new ones. Well, new used ones, I guess.
- Jackie and I are going to ask our moms to take us to the library at the same time! That way we can still be partners.

Children get good ideas from one another in these conversations, and you get the joy of watching your class community talk about their reading lives with more independence and direction than ever. You'll need to hold onto this when next year's students walk through the door and you ask yourself, "Were last year's children really this young?" They were! And your new class will grow to be just as accomplished as this year's class!

As part of saying good-bye, I like to put the sheets students have filled out for this unit into some sort of special folder or sleeve with their report cards. I make these out of pretty paper and decorate them, writing the children's names in glitter or metallic pen. It has the feeling of a diploma, and it indicates to parents that the contents are special. I want to give parents every reason to help their children read for pure entertainment.

Then I go and get started on my own summer reading! Enjoy.

Appendix A
Student Handouts

A–1 I am the kind of reader who...
A–2 Nonfiction and You!
A–3 The Reader You Are Now
A–4 Summer Reading Plan
A–5 Reading Resources

Name_____ Date_____

I am the kind of reader who...

Likes to read in this place
Likes to read this kind of book
Likes to read with these people

Figure A–1 I am the kind of reader who . . .

Nonfiction and You!

Tell me a little about yourself as a nonfiction reader. This will help me make the best decisions about what and how to teach this month.

What is one nonfiction book you have read recently?

_____
- -
_____
- -
_____

What is one thing you do when you read nonfiction that you DO NOT do when you read fiction?

_____
- -
_____
- -
_____
- -
_____
- -
_____

How do you choose a nonfiction book to read?

_____
- -
_____
- -
_____

© 2010 by Stephanie Parsons from *First Grade Readers*. Portsmouth, NH: Heinemann.

Figure A–2 Nonfiction and You!

Name_____ Date_____

Wow! I can't believe it's already the last month of school!
We have all come a long way as readers. Think about the reader
you used to be, and tell me about the reader you are now. Some
things might have changed a lot, and some things might be the
same.

I used to read this kind of book:	Now I read this kind of book:
I used to like to read in this place:	Now I like to read in this place:
I used to...	Now I...
I used to...	Now I...

Figure A–3 The Reader You Are Now

Summer Reading Plan

We have talked about different ways a book can be JUST RIGHT. This paper can help you choose books that will be just right for you to read during the summer.

Write the title of one book you know is just right for you in the box at the top of this page. Use the table below to help you plan what you want to read during the summer.

Books I want someone to read to me	
Author(s) I love or want to get to know better	
Character(s) I love or want to get to know better	
Style or Genre I enjoy	
Topic(s) I like or want to learn more about	
Series I want to explore	

Figure A–4 Summer Reading Plan

Reading Resources

Readers have lots of ways to get what they need. Use this sheet to help you get what you need as a reader this summer

Friends Who Read Similar Books

Name _____ Phone number _____

Name _____ Phone number _____

Name _____ Phone number _____

Name _____ Phone number _____

Library

Address _____ Phone number _____

_____

Story times _____

Summer Reading Programs _____

Bookstore _____

Address _____ Phone number _____

_____

Bookstore _____

Address _____ Phone number _____

_____

Websites

_____   _____

_____   _____

Figure A–5 Reading Resources

Appendix B
Websites to Help Foster Reading

This list is not exhaustive, but will get you started. New websites are created often, and an Internet search may yield new gold that just didn't exist at the time of publishing this book. If you share these resources with parents, please remind them that school is a rigorous learning environment. Children need not take spelling tests or comprehension quizzes at home. Rather, encourage them to use these resources to provide rainy-day fun (homework on sunny days should be to go out and play).

Free Websites

pbskids.org

This site has videos and games featuring some favorite characters.

bookpals.net

Sponsored by the Screen Actors Guild Foundation, bookpals is a site devoted to helping children love to read. Go online and you'll find great teaching resources, as well as fun activities for your students to try on their own.

storylineonline.net

A program also sponsored by SAG, storyline offers online video streaming of a variety of well-known actors reading stories aloud.

booknutsreadingclub.com

An online community for children to communicate about the books they love.

kidsreads.com

This site has a lot going on. There are reviews of books, interviews with authors, games, trivia, and sections just for parents and teachers.

magickeys.com/books/

There are a lot of books online, some of which have audio and some of which require reading the old-fashioned way.

brainpopjr.com

This is an educational site, organized by school subject and featuring skill-building games and some fun videos.

starfall.com

Starfall provides many activities to help children learn to use phonics.

bookadventure.com

There is information here for parents and teachers as well as for children. This is one of a very few sites I found that could help recommend books by grade level, genre, and topic of interest.

kidsites.com

Here you'll find links to a huge variety of sites for children, organized by topic and theme. This can be a great place for students to research topics of interest or to find out background information on topics they're reading about, as well as lessons and activities for teachers and parents to use.

Scholastic.com

The kids' section has fun videos and activities. The section for parents has a lot of resources and helpful advice. Here, too, children can practice reading nonfiction and researching topics that interest them, or learn more about the topics they're reading about in other books.

go-kids.grolier.com

Grolier gives online access to their children's encyclopedia, with interesting links and great pictures.

Fee-based Websites

onemorestory.com

This is an online library of well-known children's literature. Children can select a book from a large array of popular picture books. An expressive reading of each book is accompanied by wonderful music that helps set the mood for the story, and children can follow along with the words on the screen.

readinga-z.com

This is more for teachers than for parents, but many parents will want access to the materials provided here. They offer a lot of free samples of downloadable reading materials, too.

Scholastic.com

Scholastic offers a subscription service giving access to thousands of printable materials at various reading levels. This website is aimed at educators but parents might find it useful and fun. Scholastic is also responsible for BookFlix, an interactive online literacy resource. Many library systems offer free access to BookFlix for cardholders.